Lessons From a Life Lived

a Life Lived

One man's true-life stories, and the lessons they taught.

By

Charles W. Kissling

Ann & Keith,
Thank you for all
that you do.
Chuck Kissling

Dedicated to:

My wife, who perfected my Christian Faith by leading me into the Catholic Church, and who gave so much of herself in bearing and raising 3 sons. She is the personification of a Saint on earth.

My sons, each of whom is a better man than I, and who have brought me so much pride and joy.

My daughters-in-law, who are the daughters I never had.

My grandchildren, may they learn from these lessons, and remember more of their grandfather Kissling than I remember of my grandfather Kissling.

Contents

Foreword by Cory Kissling

My brother is eighteen months older than me. Like many younger brothers, I idolized him, and wanted to be just like him. It is no surprise then that we shared many of the same experiences. In this book, Chuck describes events that shaped his life. My memories of the events we shared are much the same as his. The lessons we learned, and what we took away from those experiences though, are much different. You see, as much as I wanted to be just like my brother, the reality is that we are very different people. Fortunately our parents realized that we are not the same, and therefore the lessons that we needed to learn were not the same.

Reading this reminded me of a sociology experiment that tries to determine if it is the environment or genetics that form our personality. My brother and I experienced many of the same events in our lives and yet we have different personalities. As you read this book, ask yourself if there is a lesson to be learned by you. What can I learn from this story? How would I respond? Thank you Chuck, for sharing your story.

Cory Kissling
(Little brother)

Introduction

The original intent in writing this book was simply to pass on some of the lessons I have learned in my life, and to tell the stories as to how I learned those lessons. It was never my intent to write an autobiography. I have never thought that anything I have done should warrant that anyone should write a biography of my life, and heaven forbid that I should think enough of myself to write an autobiography of my life. However, as the ideas formed in my head, and as I began to put the stories to paper, it became obvious to me that I was indeed writing what could properly be labeled as an autobiography.

As such, I ask the reader to focus on the lessons portrayed within the stories. It is these lessons that I think form the foundation and provide the importance of my written words. I hope that the reader will receive the lessons as the important part of each story, and will remember that the focus should be on the lesson, and not on me. My intent is to pass on the lessons, not to tell the story of my life.

Accidents Can Happen in the Blink of an Eye

My grandfather, Charles Kissling, died at age 65 and one month. As I write this, I am 65 and 2 months. I was four and a half years old when he died, and I have only a few certain memories of him. I have other memories of him, but I am not certain that they are true memories. Some of them, I suspect...no, I am sure, are pseudo-memories. For instance, I have this general sense that he was a gentle man, but I have no distinct memory to confirm that. I do know for certain that he cared for me. There are stories of grandpa and I that have been told to me, and having heard the stories I have created an image of them in my mind. Having heard some of the stories so many times as I grew up, and pictured them so many times in my mind, I am now left with doubt as to what is a true memory and what is a memory of what has been told to me. One memory, however, I am certain of being a true memory. I will relate that story to you later.

Having reached and surpassed the age at which grandpa died, and having so few memories of him leads me to wonder about my own grandchildren. If I were to die tomorrow, would they remember me? Would they remember the good times together? Or would they be left, as I am, with a mixture of real and pseudo memories? I trust that they will remember that I care for them, just as my grandfather cared for me. I know that real or not, and few as they are, I am thankful for the memories of Popo (that is what I called my grandfather Kissling) that I do have.

Grandpa was the first-born son of a Swiss immigrant. Great grandfather John Charles Kissling came to the USA as a young man from Basil, Switzerland. He settled in the German immigrant community of Longford, Kansas, which is about 25 miles north of Abilene, Kansas. He married the daughter of an Iroquois Indian, raised 2 sons and 3 daughters, and became a leader of the community. He farmed, owned a business and served on the School Board and on the Telephone Board.

Above: Great grandfather John Charles Kissling

My grandfather grew up helping on the farm, and at the age of 25, joined the Army and went to France to fight in World War I, the "war to end all wars". He sent many letters and post cards home from France, and amazingly those letters and post cards still exist. I have read every one of them. They are each simply addressed to John Kissling, Longford Kansas, USA. It is perhaps in reading these personal letters that I gained some sense of his character. Nearly every one, even the ones that were written while hospitalized in France, contain the words "I am fine and dandy, hope you are same." He never explained why he was in the hospital for a month, and he never discussed the war. My dad thought that his dad had developed pneumonia while in France. I think that this is a possibility, or it may be that he developed lung issues because of the poison gas that the enemy used against our troops. Grandpa did say, in his letters that he had walked all the way across France from the Atlantic shore to near the France-Germany-Switzerland border where his dad had come from (Basil, Switzerland). In the letter, he did not specifically mention Basil, because each of his letters was subject to sensor. He simply wrote, "I am within a days walk from where you came from". He also noted that he had not seen very many airplanes.

Above: Post card sent home from France, Sept. 6, 1918 by my grandfather, Charles E. Kissling

After coming home from the war, my grandfather married my grandmother, Anna, who lived in the Irish immigrant community of Idana, Kansas, which was about 15 miles north of Longford. It is interesting that the Irish and the Germans did not get along well together, so I suspect that their relationship had a little Romeo and Juliet flavor to it. They stayed on the farm with great grandpa John Charles, and had four sons born to them. My dad was the only son who survived birth. Grandma and grandpa had to have suffered much sorrow at the loss of those babies. They left Longford when my dad was 9 years old, largely driven away by two factors. First was the death of John Charles, and second was the devastation caused by the dust bowl. They moved to a farm just south of Stafford, Kansas with the hope of a fresh start. The house they lived in had electricity, but no running water. Their water was taken from a hand pumped well. Water was pumped one bucket at a time. They kept a basin of water in the house for hand and face washing. It required many buckets of water to bathe, and when we visited, my brother and I would bathe in a tub of water in the yard.

Author (rt.), brother Cory (lt.) bathing in outdoor tubs on Grandfather Kissling's farm.

Grandmother and grandfather Kissling, 1956

I distinctly remember spending the night in that house, in an upstairs bedroom. Grandpa gave me a basin to put under the bed for use during the night if I needed to go the bathroom. He did not want me to have to go outside to the outhouse in the dark. I also remember climbing the ladder on the windmill, and grandpa helping me down. I can remember riding on the combine with grandpa during wheat harvest. I have been told that grandpa enjoyed carrying me around the farm with my feet in the pockets of his over-alls. I relate these things to you in order that you, too, can have a sense of the character of my grandfather Kissling, and the life he lived.

In the summer of 1957 grandpa hooked up an electric motor to the water pump so that he did not have to pump water by hand any more. The motor powered the pump via a belt running between a pulley on the motor and a pulley on the pump. He still had to carry water into the house one bucket at a time, but he did not have to pump. With this improvement, he simply hung the bucket on the end of the pump outlet, and plugged in the pump. He was so proud of this accomplishment that when we arrived for a visit, the first thing he did was show us his new water system. I can distinctly remember standing there with my dad and his father, my grandpa. Grandpa reached up and connected the two electrical cords hanging overhead. I do not remember what happened next, however I can relate to you what has been told to me. As the motor began to turn the pulleys, and the pump began to send water into the bucket, I reached out and grabbed hold of the belt running between the two pulleys. My left hand was immediately pulled into the pulley, sending me tumbling down and around until my hand came out the other side. Neither my dad nor my grandpa could act quickly enough to prevent me from grabbing the pulley, nor quickly enough to shut off the power once I did grab hold.

My hand was a bloody, mangled mess, and a half-inch of my left index finger had been cut off. They wrapped my hand with handkerchiefs, and mom and dad rushed me into town to a doctor. The next thing I remember is the doctor saying "we'll have to cut it off", followed by my screaming. I thought he wanted to cut off my hand, but all he was saying was he needed to cut off the wrapping. I am told that he indeed thought that the best course of action was to amputate my hand, but mom and dad wanted another opinion. My hand was re-wrapped, and we returned to the farm. I have a distinct memory of our car stopping in the road as we approached the farm. Grandpa had gotten into his truck and was driving into town to see how I was doing. I remember him standing in the road looking at me through the window of the car, and I remember how devastated he looked. The home improvement that he was so proud of had been the cause of terrible harm to his grandson. That is the last memory I have of him. He died from Tetanus just a few months later, after stepping on a rusty nail.

We made the drive back to our home in Bartlesville, Oklahoma. The doctors there thought I might lose my finger, but they did not think it would be necessary to amputate the hand. I spent a little more than a year with my hand strapped to a board, much like a ping-pong paddle. Prior to the accident, I had been left-handed. With my hand strapped to the board, I was forced to use my right hand. I started Kindergarten with my hand still strapped to the board, and learned to write with my right hand. Now I am fully right handed. The left index finger remains a half inch shorter than the right index finger, and my left hand is just plain uncoordinated.

I wish that my last memory of Popo were something other than what it is. I wish it were a memory of him and I playing or laughing, or of him just holding me. But it is not. Instead, I am left with memory of a sad grandfather looking at me with such care and sorrow in his face. Perhaps that contributes to my general sense that he was a gentle man, because a gentle man is also a caring man.

I wish that he had lived long enough to know that the injury did not stop me from growing into a functioning adult and father. I wish he knew that the worse thing to come from the accident was that I grew up right handed instead of left handed.

My grandpa, my dad, and myself all learned a valuable lesson that day: accidents can happen in the blink of an eye, children will grab hold of anything, and they need constant supervision. The truth is, I am sure grandpa already knew that. He had successfully raised my father. On that horrible day, however, he was reminded of that lesson and the constant need to keep an eye on the kids, especially when there is dangerous equipment nearby. This lesson, however, was a first for me. Children are so curious and inquisitive that they will grab or touch just about anything that draws their interest. What may draw the interest of a child is not necessarily what draws the interest of an adult. I was more interested in the spinning belt than I was in the running water that held the attention of my dad and my grandpa. I imagine that after the accident grandpa made some kind of protective cover for the belt and pulleys so that an accident like mine would not happen again.

As adults, the best we can do is to keep diligent watch over our children. It is impossible to keep constant watch over them, and to observe every move they make. So we try to anticipate what harm they might get into, and create barriers or other means of protecting them and preventing the harm. We do things such as putting childproof locks on any cabinet containing cleaning supplies or other chemicals holding potential harm to a curious child. We also put plastic covers over electrical outlets to prevent a child from inserting something into the outlet and receiving an electrical shock. These things are easier to remember and anticipate for parents with young children in the house constantly. It is harder for grandparents, who may not have had young children in the house for 20 years. In the last 8 years, I have had to re-child proof my house. All of the cabinet locks had long since been removed but are now back in place. As careful as we are, however, accidents will still happen. We hope and pray that when they do, the results are not tragic.

Fifty-five years after the accident, God opened my eyes to recognize how much one of my patients resembles my grandfather. Now, every time I see this man I am reminded of my grandfather and a smile forms deep in my soul.

Actions Have Consequences

As a young child, not yet of school age, my hair was generally cut short in such a manner as to require little or no combing or styling. Dad would sit my brother and I down and use the hair clippers to cut our hair as needed. Once I started school, my hair was allowed to grow some and my mother combed my hair. The routine included "a little dab" of Brylcreem rubbed into my hair, followed by the act of combing and styling my hair. The Brylcreem advertisements promised that "a little dab'll do ya, or watch out, the girls will all pursue ya". The style probably varied from day to day, or week to week, or even season to season. I say this because it was tradition that my brother and I would receive a buzz hair cut every summer.

As I got older, I came to be in charge of the Brylcreem application and the combing of my own hair. Even though I combed my hair, my mom still determined the style. Generally this meant a part on the left side, the top combed flat and to the right, and the front combed up and back to the right, keeping it off of my forehead. I had some artistic control, in that I could adjust the flip of the front hair, but that was the extent of my input. I even carried a black comb in my back pocket. I am not sure that there was any practical purpose for that comb, because if I used enough Brylcreem, hurricane strength winds would not have messed my hair enough to require re-combing. Perhaps more to the point, it was a statement of style to have a comb sticking out of your jeans pocket. When summer arrived, out came the clippers and we received our summer buzz cut. Here again, we had little input, although I do remember requesting a flattop cut rather than a full buzz cut. It must be recognized that there is really only very little difference between a full buzz cut and a flat top cut. The flat top cut, however, allowed me to use a little hair wax on the hair at the front, combing it straight up. Yes sir, I was quite stylish. Plenty of hair grease with hair combed up and back off the forehead, and then summer buzz or flattop.

In the fifth grade, approaching eleven years old, I began to think that I had more control over my hairstyle. It occurred to me that maybe, just maybe, I had complete and total control. Maybe I possessed creative license over my own hair. My brother, a year and a half younger, did not have such illusion. He knew that the creative control still resided fully and solely with mom and dad, and he was smart enough to know not to question that control.

In February of 1964, while I was in the fifth grade, the Beatles first appeared on the Ed Sullivan show. Not only did the Beatles usher in a new era of music, but also hairstyle. They sported what was called a mop top haircut. Their hair was combed down onto the forehead, and was allowed to hang over the tops of their ears. This was unheard of at the time. Very quickly, boys began to comb their hair down onto the forehead in an effort to mimic the Beatles.

While walking to school one morning, I decided to exercise creative control over my own hair. I pulled the comb out of my pocket, and quickly combed my hair down onto my forehead, Brylcreem and all. Can you picture that? The Brylcreemed hair plastered flat against my forehead must have been quite a site. My brother, knowing where the true creative control lay, could not stop himself from blurting out, "I'm going to tell mom!" This is not to suggest that my brother was a "tattle-tale". I had said the same thing to him many times for other reasons. Such is the nature of brothers, quick to bring to light any behavior by the other which might be contrary to the parents desires. Of course, on the way home from school, I combed my hair back to the approved style. Even though I felt I could determine my own hairstyle, I was not quite ready to flout it in front of my mom.

As you can guess, mom and dad were not happy about my attempt at non-conformity. Nobody but the Beatles combed their hair down on the forehead, and the Beatles were not to be admired or followed. After all, the music they played was not the kind of music to be listened to. In short, the Beatles were trouble and were not to be imitated. Very quickly, I don't recall exactly when (it may have even been that very evening), I received my summer buzz cut early. That put an immediate end to my hairstyle rebellion.

As I got older, I was gradually allowed to comb my hair as I wanted. Never so much down my forehead, but at least not combed back and away. Once I reached college age, I guess mom and dad decided I could make some decisions on my own, so I pretty much threw caution to the wind. Never becoming a true "long hair", but I thought I was quite daring to allow my hair to cover my ears, hang onto my collar in the back, and go wherever it wanted to up front. Looking back now, that seems a bit reserved and tame compared to what it could have been. I attribute that to the strong foundation that my parents laid for me to follow. There were reasons they wanted to keep my appearance acceptable to not only them, but to society in general. They never spelled out those reasons to me, rather allowing me to reach the proper conclusions on my own, knowing that a conclusion reached on my own would stand up to the test of life's experiences better than one that they hammered into me. One of those conclusions was the simple recognition that if I wanted to have a job, I must keep a respectable and presentable appearance.

Yes, I eventually had the freedom to exercise complete and total artistic control over my own hairstyle and appearance. At the same time, I learned that with freedom comes responsibility, and that there were consequences for my actions.

Obey Your Mother

Mom wasn't what you would call a small woman, but standing only about 5'3" she was anything but tall. In spite of her size, she was not to be dismissed. Her paternal grandmother had raised her along with her two older brothers. This was because her mother died from complications related to childbirth about 6 weeks after giving birth to my mother. Hence, mom never knew her mother, and carried a certain amount of guilt with her for the rest of her life. She felt that her mom would not have died if she had never been born. How sad. Survivor's guilt can be hard to fully be rid of once it takes hold, no matter how irrational it may be. Her childhood was not particularly happy, as her grandmother was demanding and strict. So she grew up without her mother, and with a father who travelled extensively, and was raised by her grandmother.

Above: Grandmother Nettie Euwer, my mom's mother, who died 6 weeks after giving birth to my mom.

Above: My mom being held by her grandmother Euwer, who raised her. Also, her grandfather Euwer and her two brothers Harold and Charles.

World War II began while mom was in the 9th grade. Each of her two older brothers enlisted as soon as they could after graduation from high school, one in the Navy and one in the Army Air Corp. Soon, they were both in harms way. Mom sewed two blue stars onto cloth to be displayed in the window of their home. The blue star on display in the window signified that a service member had come from that home and was serving in our country's Armed Forces. In mom's case, 2 stars meant 2 service members. Homes all over the country had these Service Flags displayed in their windows.

On July 7, 1944, just weeks after she graduated from high school, her older brother Charles was killed in Germany. His B24 bomber crashed in the early morning 2K south of the town of Egeln in northeast Germany. The family received notice that he was missing in action some time after that, and eventually notice that he was dead. Mom did the only thing she could do at the time. She sewed a gold star over one of the blue stars. The gold star signified that the service member had died while in the service. Later in life, mom tearfully told me the story of sewing the gold star onto the Service Flag in the window. She had been reminded of that gold star on the day that I pinned a small gold star onto her blouse when I received the rank of Star Scout in the Boy Scouts.

Above: The Service Flag that hung in the window of my mom's house during WWII. Notice the upper star has had a gold star sewn over the blue star, signifying the death of Charles.

Above: My mother in her WWII WACS uniform.

Wanting to do her part for the country, mom joined the WACS (Women's Auxiliary Corp) and served as a switchboard operator at the Goodyear Tire Plant in Topeka. She wore a uniform and had some basic self-defense training. I was not to learn of this training until my early teenage years.

Sometime around the age of 12 or 13 years old, I came to the realization that I had grown taller than my mom. I imagine that she may have been the first to bring it to my attention, as parents are wont to do, with a certain amount of pride in their children. I don't have a memory of her telling me that I was taller, but I remember telling each of my son's that very thing when they surpassed me. And I remember the pride with which I told them. I imagine mom felt the same pride. I don't know that it meant that much to me, in as much as I was still one of the shorter kids in my class at school. No one in our family was what you would call tall, although my paternal Grandfather was six feet tall.

About this same age, I was beginning to feel a certain amount of independence, and along with that independence a certain amount of rebelliousness to authority. I think all kids go through this period, suddenly realizing that they have some control over what they do and when they do it, rather than just being told what and when. The day came when mom asked me to do something in the house. What I was asked to do, I have no memory. What I clearly remember is saying <u>no</u> to her. And not only telling her no, but when she asked a second time, telling her that she could not make me do it because I was bigger than her. That was the moment when I found out that mom had learned some self defense skills, and that she had not forgotten them.

She quietly walked up to me, stood at my side and put an arm on my shoulder. Then as quick as lightning she put a foot forward positioning it just behind me, and simultaneously turned her body away from mine, pushing with her arm on my shoulder, and flipped me harmlessly over her hip onto the floor. In the blink of an eye, I found myself on the floor at my mother's feet, looking up at her with her hands on her hips. She had performed a flawless hip throw. Looking down at me she said, "You may be bigger than me, but I can still put you on the floor, and you will do what I ask you to do!" Then she quietly walked away, and I lay there trying to figure out what just happened. Later in life, she would occasionally remind me of that incident and tell me that she could do it all over again if she needed to. I never tested that hypothesis.

That is when I learned that my mom was tough, even if she was not big in stature, and that I should obey my mother. I cannot remember ever wantonly disobeying my mother again. My mom had been made tough by a number of trials in her life. Growing up not knowing her mother and carrying guilt that she was the cause of her mother's death; being raised by a strict grandmother along with 2 older brothers; having a father largely absent from the home; watching both brothers go off to war; changing one of the blue service stars to gold upon the death of one brother; then doing what she could for our country's war effort by joining the WAC's. Her High School Yearbook is a sad testament to the sorrows of the time. My mom scribbled notes next to the pictures of nearly half of the boys in her graduating class; notes such as "killed in action, Europe", or "killed in action, Pacific", or "missing in action". Graduation from High School should be a memorable part of one's life because of the joy of the present, and the dreams of potential yet to be developed. Mom's generation had no such joy, and far too many lives were cut short, not seeing those dreams come to fruition.

Mom was never able to visit the grave of her brother, Charles. The people of Egeln, Germany buried him and the other members of his flight crew in the town cemetery. They marked the graves, and kept records of the burials. Enemies though they were, the German people still demonstrated basic human decency in this act. After the war ended, Germany turned over all of the burial records to U.S. grave recovery teams. Charles' body was recovered by one of the these teams, and his family was given the option of bringing him home to the U.S., or re-burying him in one of the American Cemeteries that were being created in Europe. He was eventually buried in the Ardennes American Cemetery in Belgium, along with more than 5,000 other U.S. Military members. I was blessed to be able to visit his grave in 2016, it was the least I could do for an Uncle I never met; an Uncle who had given his life in the battle against evil, so that one-day others might live in a better world. It was the least I could do for my mother, who had endured so much sorrow, and in her own way taught me to obey.

Above: Grave of Charles T. Euwer, Jr.
Ardennes American Cemetery, Belgium

Thou Shall Not Curse

In the summer of 1969 the Viet Nam War was raging, and every evening the nightly news reported the daily body count from the war. Eighteen year olds were registering for the draft, and anti-war rallies were staged frequently. In the midst of the war turmoil, however, was great hope and adventure as the USA sent men to the moon for the first time in human history. I was 16 years old, trying to figure out who I was and who I was destined to be, and working for the summer as a counselor at Boy Scout Camp Tawakoni. This was a camp for Boy Scouts to spend a week camping and learning skills and earning badges. Among the skills learned were camping, swimming, canoeing, sailing, row boating, and nature. My job was to teach camping skills. I taught scouts how to set up and take down a tent, where to put a tent and where not to put it. I also taught them how to start a fire. What I especially enjoyed teaching them, however, was tying knots. I had learned knot tying from my dad, who had learned to tie many knots while in the Navy during WWII. He taught me tips to help tying knots such as a square knot is tied "right over left, left over right". The bowline knot is tied as "the squirrel comes out of the hole, around the tree, and back into the hole". A taut-line hitch is tied "two in, one out".

That summer I was also learning that a 16 year old is not a child any more, and yet not quite an adult. In the evenings, the camp staff members would gather. That is when we jockeyed for position within the social order, much like male gorillas jockey for position within their social order. The higher in the social order of the staff, the more "cool" one was, the more respected one was, and the more admired one was. Our jockeying consisted mostly of demonstrations of physical prowess (arm wrestling, boxing), story telling about cars and girls, and cursing.

I was pretty much a "nerd" in school, making good grades, not terribly athletic, and wearing black plastic glasses with thick lenses. I terribly wanted to be seen by my fellow counselors, who were all male and generally 15-18 years old, as something other than a nerd. Having just turned 16, I did not have very much driving experience, did not own a car, and hence had no car stories to exaggerate. Likewise, I had no girl stories to share. I was only of average physical size, but I did have one physical attribute that I could use to my advantage in the struggle to rise beyond nerd hood in the social order. I had extremely strong stomach muscles, which I had developed by doing sit-ups daily. As such, I could harden my stomach and receive any blow that even the largest boys could deliver. In addition, while the others would demonstrate strength by breaking tree limbs over their knees, I broke those same limbs against my stomach. These feats earned me the knick name of iron belly. I am not sure that any of this lifted me out of nerd status, though, because stomach strength was not as "cool" as arm strength. Perhaps, to the contrary, it rather only served to cement my status as a nerd, because breaking branches against one's stomach is probably just plain weird.

Thus, the only tool left to me in my struggle to rise in the social order was cursing. Some of the boys, especially the older boys, were very adept at cursing. The more frequently that one uttered a curse word, or the more shocking the word, the higher in the social order one could rise. It was "cool" to curse. I had not been exposed to very much cursing until that point in my life. Other than an occasional expletive, I do not recall my dad ever cursing. So, in the company of the other counselors, during our private time in the evenings, I began to learn to curse. We walked a bit of a tightrope as far as cursing is concerned, in that it was absolutely forbidden to curse in front of the scouts we instructed.

Any cursing had to be kept strictly among the staff, and well out of earshot of any campers. I was pretty good at managing my own language, limiting any curse words to be uttered only in the evenings during our staff social time. As the summer progressed, so did my cursing skills. To this day, I am not sure that any of this actually elevated me in the pecking order of our social structure, but at the time I convinced myself that I was not a nerd, and was actually a member of the cool guys.

One might be tempted to think that this was just a group of bad boys, not the boys that parents would want for friends to their children. That would be a wrong assumption. These were just boys caught in that period of life where they are no longer children, and yet not quite men either. We were all struggling to navigate the perilous path from childhood to manhood, trying to negotiate the forks in the road of life. Trying to learn good from bad, good behavior from bad behavior, good actions from bad actions, good choices from bad choices and the consequences that will inevitably accompany those choices. Most of these boys were Eagle Scouts, good students, patriotic, and were generally the type of boy that parents want their daughters to marry. My good friend and tent mate, Randy, finished college in 4 years, and became an award winning photojournalist. Another staff member, Neal, would attend the Air Force Academy a year later; and while serving in the Air Force in 1979 he was taken and held hostage at the American Embassy in Tehran during the Iran Hostage Crisis. He later retired as a Brigadier General. Both of these boys successfully navigated the boy to man path, grew into respected men, married and stayed married to the same woman until their deaths at age 63 and age 65 respectively. Cursing did not define them. It was simply an attempt to move from childhood to manhood, an experiment in routing much like one experiments with which route to take from one place to another. Some routes are quickly abandoned.

Every four years, the Boy Scouts of America host a National Jamboree. 1969 was the year for Jamboree to be held in Farragut State Park, Idaho. Approximately 34,000 scouts from all over the country were to attend the Jamboree in late July, and I was fortunate enough to be among them. Prior to the Jamboree, our local group had some planning and organizing to do. We were organized into two troops, each made up of about 32 scouts aged 14-18. Each troop was broken down into 4 patrols of 8 scouts each. Because I was an Eagle Scout, and had demonstrated leadership skills, and was actively working at a Boy Scout camp, I was chosen to be a patrol leader. This meant that I was responsible for leading 7 other scouts during the Jamboree.

As part of the planning, we were to hold a practice overnight campout at Camp Tawakoni. So, in the middle of July, the members of our Jamboree Troop arrived at Tawakoni early on a Saturday afternoon, after the campers of the week had gone home. After finishing my counselor duties for the week, I joined the Jamboree Troop, and was introduced to the 7 other members of my patrol. None of us knew each other, and I was nervous. I wanted to make a good impression on them, and to demonstrate to them that there was a reason I was appointed to be their patrol leader. The first task to be accomplished, after introductions, was to set up our tents. I carefully explained the general tent arrangement for our patrol, and showed where each tent was to be placed. The tents were the type known as "wall tents", each having 8 guy ropes attaching the tent to stakes in the ground. Each guy rope had a taut line hitch (knot) tied on it, creating a loop to be placed around the ground stake. The significance of this particular knot is that it can be slid up and down the rope to tighten or loosen the tent's connection to the ground stake. Most of the ropes already had the taut line hitch tied, so it was only necessary to drive a stake into the ground and then place the rope loop over the stake and adjust the tension of the rope. We worked in four pairs, each pair setting up a tent. I occasionally walked away from my tent to monitor the progress of the other pairs setting up their tents. One of the scouts pointed out that a rope on his tent did not have a knot tied on it. I replied, "just tie a taut line hitch on it." He responded, "I don't know how to tie a taut line hitch."

That is when it happened. I lost control, and let loose with a profanity-laced tirade that would make a drunken sailor proud. "What the H--- do you mean, you don't know how to tie a f------ taut line hitch? Holy sh--! How the f--- did you ever become a First Class Scout if you can't tie a G—D--- taut line? It's f------- simple, just two in, and one out! Here, give me the G—D--- rope and I will f------ tie it for you!" Then I looked at him. He did not say a word; he just stood there trembling, with a look of pure horror and shock on his face. At that moment, I saw myself through his eyes, and I was just as shocked as he was. What had I become? The person I saw through this boy's eyes was not the person I wanted to be. I was ashamed of what I saw. I do not recall what I did next. Did I apologize? Did I simply tie the knot and walk away? I do not know.

What I do know is that I never again let forth such a stream of profanity from my mouth. I might be able to count on my fingers the number of times I have since used the "f" word. Yes, I will still cry out d--- or sh-- if I hit my thumb with a hammer, or stub a toe while walking barefoot through the dark house. Even yelling d----, d----, d---- when I hit the outside mirror of the truck against the garage wall while backing out. I suppose I am only human. But never again has a profanity-laced tirade escaped my lips.

As I reflect back on this incident, I believe that not only did I see myself through the eyes of that scout, I saw myself through the eyes of God. Not only did I see myself through His eyes, but I saw God's reaction displayed on the face of a boy. God used that scout to show me His reaction to my behavior and language: disappointment and horror. That is the only explanation for such a profound and sudden impact on my life. After all, if it was simply that I saw myself through the eyes of another boy, I would think I should have been somewhat proud and impressed with myself. After all, that was the whole purpose wasn't it? Had not my goal been to raise my standing in the male youth social order? Such a response from a peer should have been confirmation of my elevation above nerd hood. I should have seen myself as above this scout. Instead, what I saw made me feel anything but proud. I felt truly ashamed, and it changed my life instantly.

Yes, sometimes God allows us, or rather forces us, to see our selves through His eyes in the faces of other people. We may not like what we see. Even more profound, however, is when He allows us to see His face displayed through the face of another person. That can be life changing. It certainly was for me.

Make the Time

In the summer of 1974 I took a motorcycle trip. Leaving Minnesota I went south through Iowa, through Missouri and into Kansas where I visited my friend from Boy Scouts, Randy. Then I headed east across Missouri and into Indiana. Heading north I visited some childhood friends living in Michigan. Turning west, I arrived at Luddington, Michigan. Luddington is a town on the eastern shore of Lake Michigan, and is the home of a ferry that travels west across the Lake to Wisconsin.

The Luddington-Manitowoc Ferry travels the 60-mile width of Lake Michigan in about 4 hours, and can carry automobiles on it. Driving from Luddington to Manitowoc is a distance of more than 400 miles. I could choose to take the ferry, and be in Manitowoc by 10PM, or spend the night in Luddington and ride to Manitowoc the next day, arriving sometime in the afternoon. It seemed to me that taking the ferry would save me a day of travel on my way home.

Boarding the ferry, motorcycles were placed in an area of their own, off to the side of the cars and trucks. I parked my bike next to two other motorcycles. I got a bite to eat in the canteen, and then went for a walk on deck. I had never been on a body of water as large as

Lake Michigan before, and soon could not see anything but water in any direction. I was having the time of my life. As it got dark I headed inside to find a seat for the remainder of the journey.

I saw two men, probably 15 years older than I, who looked like they were motorcycle riders (the helmets they were carrying gave them away). I sat down across from them and struck up a conversation. You know the type of conversation that occurs between strangers finding themselves to be fellow travelers. "Where are you headed? Where have you been? What kind of bike are you riding? How is the ride on that machine?" I quickly learned that each of these men had a daughter riding with them. They explained that during the riding season, every six weeks they take a 3 or 4-day trip together, each bringing a different family member. The wives got a turn, and each of the children got a turn going on these trips. I remarked how nice that was, and then I asked, "How do you ever find the time to take a trip every 6 weeks?" The reply that instantly came back to me was a piece of wisdom that I have never forgotten. One of the men said, "If we waited until we could find the time, it would never be there. We make the time!"

Wow! These men made the time for themselves, and they made the time for their families. How often do we find ourselves saying "I just don't have the time", or "If I could only find the time"? We can all learn from this wisdom. Anything that is truly important to us deserves that we make the time for it. Anyone who is truly important to us deserves that we make the time for him or her. If we wait until we find the time, it will never be there. Something else will always get in the way. We all live busy lives, and there is always something to do or someplace to go. The things and people that matter most to us get swamped and over run by the busyness of our lives unless we take deliberate action. We must set our priorities, and then make time for those priorities. If we do not make the time for something or someone, it can't really be a priority. Figure out what, and especially who, is really important to you and then make the time for them. You won't regret it. I don't think a dying man ever said, "I wish I hadn't spent so much time with my loved ones."

Never Point a Weapon at Another Person

It was September 1975. I was canoeing in the waters bordering Minnesota and Canada with my friend, Rick. The Boundary Waters, in my opinion, is one of the most beautiful places in the world. I grew up in Kansas, only moving to Minnesota in my junior year of high school. When I first saw the Boundary Waters, I was impressed by the beauty, the trees, the lakes and streams, and perhaps most by the first true wilderness that I had ever seen. A person growing up in Kansas does not have it in his visual vocabulary to even just imagine what this vast wilderness is like. The forest of densely packed trees is only interrupted by the thousands of lakes in the area. The lakes range in size from very small to very large. The water is so clear that you can see rocks on the lake bottom 6-10 feet below the water's surface. It is so clean that you can safely drink the water straight from the lake.

The only lakes that allow motorboats are on the very edges of the area. Once you get away from the edge lakes, canoes are the transportation of choice. There are no roads between the lakes, only foot trails that are called portages. A portage can be as short as 50 yards, or as long as several miles. The portages are rugged, rocky, and wind through the trees. Most of them start with a short,

steep climb away from the lake, and end with a
short steep drop down to the next lake.

Rick and I were travelling in one canoe, and
carrying a pack full of food for 2 weeks, a pack
containing a tent and cooking gear, and a pack
containing our sleeping bags and clothing and
other personal gear. As the days went by, and we
consumed each day's food, the food pack became
lighter and lighter. Eventually we were able to
combine the food and equipment into one pack.
Most people think that it takes two persons to carry
a canoe, but this is not necessarily true. The
canoes used in the Boundary Waters have a yoke
in the center, connected to the port (left) and
starboard (right) gunwales (the edges of the
canoe). The yoke has two pads made to rest on
one's shoulders. Thus, one person can carry the
canoe, balanced on his shoulders. There is an art
to picking the canoe up and getting it onto your
shoulders, but with practice it becomes reasonably
easy. Easy that is for the young and strong. I
think that I would struggle with it now, although
proper technique can go a long way to reducing the
amount of strength required. I have hoisted a
canoe to my shoulders so many times that I think
the technique would still be there, even if my
strength has waned. Remember that this is true
wilderness. It is possible to get a canoe so deep
into the area that emergency help is days away.
Also, recognize that the canoe is your lifeline out
of the wilderness. Thus, we protected that canoe

very carefully. Upon arrival at the shore and beginning of a portage, we got out of the canoe while still in the water, rather than risking damage to the bottom of the canoe by running it onto the rocks of the shore. That meant stepping out into knee or hip deep water. Because of this, our boots were constantly wet. We chose to wear "jungle boots", which were designed to be worn by the military in Viet Nam. The boot had a canvas upper, and drain holes to allow water to drain. It was a luxury to put on dry socks and dry boots in the morning. Most mornings we did not have that luxury.

The portages are difficult enough that you do not want to have to walk it twice, so you do what you must in order to carry everything in one trip. This meant that one of us carried the canoe, while also carrying the personal pack on his back. The other person carried the food pack on his back, and the equipment pack on his front, and the paddles in his hands. We alternated loads with each portage. We started paddling early in the morning, and paddled most of the day, stopping to set up camp and cook dinner before it got dark. Since we were traveling in September, which is not prime time in the Boundary Waters because of colder weather, we never had trouble finding an open campsite. (In fact, we spent one day paddling with snow falling on us. We did not have winter clothing, and were forced to put socks on our hands to act as gloves.) Camping is restricted to specified Forrest

Service sites, and during prime season it can be hard to find an unoccupied campsite. Not being forced to look for a campsite earlier in the day, we were able to keep paddling until about an hour and a half before dark. Each night we took turns with the necessary chores. One of us gathered wood, started a fire and cooked. The other sat up the tent, and hung the food pack up in a tree so that it would be out of reach of a bear. There was usually some time for fishing or relaxing while the food cooked.

The first day, we put the canoe into the water of Moose Lake, and headed east. By evening we had reached Knife Lake. I took care of setting up the tent and hung the food pack after Rick had removed from the pack what he needed for dinner. He started a fire and began to prepare dinner. I took off my wet boots, and placed them next to the fire to dry a little, and put on a pair of tennis shoes. Grabbing my fishing pole, I walked about a hundred yards down the shoreline to fish. Suddenly, Rick yelled, "Your boots are on fire!" I ran as fast as I could along the rocky shoreline back to camp. I found Rick laughing, and my boots were fine. After letting him hear a little bit of my displeasure, I returned to fishing. A short while later, Rick called, "There's a bear in our camp." Sensing a little bit of "The Boy Who Cried Wolf", I kept fishing. Soon, Rick's voice carried the sound of panic. Still I fished, not bothering to answer, not wishing to interrupt my fishing. I began to hear the sound of banging pots and pans. I decided to check out the commotion. Upon reaching camp, I saw a bear standing on its rear legs and chewing on the bottom of our food pack. I began to help with the noise making, and we managed to run the bear off and back into the woods. After eating dinner, and deciding that it would be best if we did not spend the night there, we threw everything into the canoe and headed out into the darkening evening. Our map indicated a camping site on an island about a quarter mile off shore, directly across from our camp, so we headed there. Arriving at the shore, we could see someone else already camping there. They had heard our banging and yelling and were wondering if we had a bear in our camp. Very graciously, they offered to allow us to share the campsite with them for the night.

Waking early the next morning, we ate a quick breakfast and thanked the couple that shared their campsite with us. Then it was another day of paddling. That evening it was my turn to cook. Rick decided that we needed some protection, so while I prepared dinner he made a bow and arrow using a tree branch, some string, a 2 foot long straight piece of branch, and an arrowhead he had fashioned from a rock. Somehow, he thought this would be useful if we had another bear in our camp. Once it was put together, he began to practice shooting the arrow. The arrow never went far. It tended to go ten feet, then nose dive into the ground. He kept trying. I began to laugh and to teasingly suggest to him that his bow and arrow would not be very much help against a bear. Back to my cooking, I heard Rick call my name. I looked up. He was 10 yards away, with the arrow drawn, and pointing directly at me. I laughed. He released the arrow, and for the first and only time, that arrow flew straight and true. I ducked, but not quickly enough. The arrow glanced off of the overturned canoe I was using as a preparation table, and hit me square in the middle of my forehead. I fell over onto my back, mostly a result of shock and not so much because of the force of impact. Rick came running to me, apologizing profusely. Fortunately, Rick was not skilled at making a sharp arrowhead out of rock. I only suffered with a lump and bruise on my forehead. He felt so badly that he heaved both the bow and the arrow as far out into the lake as he could. We spent two full weeks in the Boundary Waters on that trip, did not see any more people and did not have any more bear trouble.

We were both lucky on that day. That arrow could just as easily hit me in the eye and caused significant harm. Any weapon should be taken seriously, something neither of us had done on that day. Every child is told not to shoot anything at another person. As adults, we know that a weapon should only be pointed at another person when harm is intended. On that day, we learned that any weapon, even a homemade weapon, is capable of causing harm, and should never be pointed at another person.

If You Want to Save Money

My first year and a half of college was
characterized by a lack of drive, motivation, and
commitment on my part. I grew up with the
understanding that after high school I would go
to college. Once there however, I floundered.
Yes, I attended class, listened carefully, and took
notes. Somehow I thought that should be
enough. It certainly had been all that was
required of me in high school, and it served me
well enough to graduate with honors. As it is,
that is not enough in college, especially not in a
college the size of the University of Minnesota.
In my first quarter (the U of M used a "quarters"
system rather than semesters; the school year
consisted of three ten-week quarters rather
than two 15-week semesters) I took Chemistry
I, Biology I, Pre-Calculus, and Freshman English.
The Chemistry class had several hundred
students seated in a theatre type class room,
trying to hear the Professor and understand his
heavy German accent while trying to see and
copy what he drew on the chalk board. The
Biology class similarly had several hundred
students in it, but did not have a live in person
instructor. Rather, there were multiple
television sets lining the outer walls of the
theatre. At the appointed time, the televisions
automatically came on and we were presented

with a taped lecture given by a professor who made no attempt to make his presentation interesting. If I had a question, too bad. There was no physical way of asking it, or of receiving an answer. Needless to say, this was not what I had experienced in school thus far, and it was not what I had expected. I did not do as well as I should have, and my path ahead became unclear. The succeeding quarters were only minimally better, and the path ahead only became even murkier.

I continued to work part time at McDonald's throughout that first year and a half. In the middle of my second year, I decided that I should take a break from college, work full time, and save some money. I needed a hiatus from college. Perhaps then I could go back to college with a greater degree of commitment and purpose. Immediately I became an assistant Manager at the McDonald's where I had worked for the prior two and a half years. Within a few months, the Head Manager quit and I was named Head Manager. Along with the new title came a larger paycheck. It did not take long before I was spending every penny I made. I bought a used 1968 GTO, a motorcycle, bought pizza for my co-workers, and generally lived large.

It did not take long for me to realize that I did not want to work at McDonald's for the rest of my life, even if it would have provided a decent income. I just did not feel fulfilled, and I did not think that it was the best use of the talents that I sensed God had given me. I quickly decided that this was to be a temporary job for me, and that I should keep college in my future plans. Thus, the first part of my hiatus plan had come to fruition: I was finding a new sense of motivation and purpose. The second part, however, that of saving some money, was not going so well.

After coming to the realization that I was not saving any money, I decided that I should invest in the stock market. I told my dad this, and he responded that he did not know anything about investing in the stock market. He did, however, know a guy who could help. So one evening he took me to visit a stockbroker at a major investing firm. I told the broker that I had $75 I wanted to invest in the stock market, maybe in McDonalds stock. He began to ask me some questions about my goals, how long I would work before going back to school, what I wanted to study, and how much money I had in savings outside of the amount I wanted to invest in the market. When I answered that I had no other savings, and that therein was the reason I wanted to invest. He sat back in his chair, looked at me and said, "If you ever want to save any money, you have to learn how to live off of less money than you earn".

I was stunned by the simple truth of that statement! I had never given any thought to how I was going to actually have the money to save or even invest. I just had a plan for what I would do with that money. I had plans for money that I did not have, because I was spending every penny I earned. How could I put money into a savings account or into the stock market if I spent the money on something else first? My eyes were suddenly opened as to the financial reality of the stockbroker's simple statement. If I was going to save some money, or invest some money for college, then I was going to have to stop spending so much. Simple, right?

It certainly would seem so, but the reality is much different. I, along with many people, did not find it so simple. Discipline is required, and discipline is sometimes hard to obtain. We all fight the battle of "wants vs. needs". What we want is not always the same as what we need. We want many things, and there is always something more to be wanted. Our wants are infinite. Our needs, on the other hand, are not infinite. We need much less than we might realize. I wanted both a motorcycle and a car, but I did not need both.

As much as I tried to change my spending habits, and save money for college, I still failed to save what I should have been able to. When it came to battling my wants, I was weak. I never really learned how to put this principle of spending less than I earned until I married my wife. We had two incomes, and I had sold my GTO in order to buy a newer, fancier sports car. So I bought a Datsun 280Z. Meanwhile my wife, Ellie, was driving a Ford Pinto. In spite of the fact that I earned more than she did, her Pinto was paid for, and I had a loan on my 280Z. Also, she had more money in savings than I. My eyes were painfully opened to my own spending habits and my failure to spend less than I earned.

She taught me a simple method to accomplish the goal of spending less than I earned. Every two weeks, we stood in line to receive our paychecks. Yes, we were actually received a paper paycheck, and had to physically take it to the bank to deposit it into our account. Ellie suggested that as soon as we had deposited our checks into our checking account, we should write ourselves a check and then deposit that check into our savings account. Money was not to be removed from the savings account except for an emergency. We were then forced to live on the money in our checking account, which meant that we were living on less than the amount we had earned. I was skeptical at first, but soon found this method to be quite effective, and surprisingly painless. I came to not miss the money that we were putting into savings, and we had as much money as we needed for our true needs. Our savings account grew steadily, and we did not miss that money. Yes, the wants were still there, but the money to pay for those wants was not readily available since it had already been set aside for saving. Simple, right? Apparently not. CNBC and USA Today, among others, reported in 2018 that 31% of Americans have less than $5000 saved for retirement. Obviously, I am not the only person to struggle with this concept of saving by living off of less money than you earn.

So, if you ever want to save any money, you have to live off of less than what you earn. A good way to do that is to immediately take a portion of your earnings and put it into savings. Then leave it there. In addition to that, if your job has a retirement plan such as a 401K or a Simple IRA, take advantage of it. That money is automatically taken from your earnings and deposited before it is paid to you. Plus, that money is put into your retirement account before any taxes have been taken out. If you follow both strategies that I have described, you will be saving for retirement and will be saving for emergency. How easy is that?! Don't let yourself be in that 31%. Live off of less than you earn, you will not regret it.

Beauty is in the Eye of the Beholder

My dad and I were out for a leisurely ride in my car one evening. You know the type. No where in particular to go, just driving around, talking at times and being quiet at times. More than anything, just enjoying each other's company.

I saw a pickup truck with a topper over the bed of the truck. It wasn't an ordinary topper. At the front, it came to be flush with the roof of the truck cab. Rearward however, it sloped down to the level of the tailgate. The sides of the topper angled inward as the surface sloped down, leaving a shape that resembled an old boat tail style car. I remarked to my dad, "that is the ugliest topper I have ever seen." He very gently replied to me, "Don't you think someone is very proud of that topper?" He did not castigate me for my insensitivity. He did not tell me that I should realize that my tastes might be different from those of another person. He simply spoke those gentle words to me and let me silently punish myself.

It is true that beauty is in the eye of the beholder. What I saw as an ugly truck topper, someone else saw as a very nice topper on his or her truck. A topper, that very likely just as my dad had said, they were quite proud of.

How easy it is for me to be critical of, and to express dislike of the appearance of many different things. Things such as the color of a house or a car, or an individual's hairstyle, or the choice of clothing worn by someone. My dad reminded that what my eyes saw as anything less than beautiful was seen as very beautiful in the eyes of another person.

I can remember a time while in college when I was very happy with my long hair, covering my ears and often uncombed. Now I wonder how many people looked at me and judged me to be a disheveled mess. I had a black "leisure suit" that I wore with a bright Hawaii style silk shirt. I thought that I looked pretty spiffy when I wore that outfit. The "leisure suit" never gained a great deal of popularity and was only around for a couple of years. Apparently, more people did not think the "leisure suit" to be as stylish as I did. Hence, today very few people remember what a "leisure suit" was. What I saw as a thing of beauty, others did not. Today, the "leisure suit" that I cherished so much is sold in costume stores. Yes, what I saw as beautiful and stylish is now the subject of laughter and is best worn as a Halloween costume.

Indeed, beauty is in the eye of the beholder. As difficult as it may be for us to remember that fact, we do well to remember it.

Sometimes we are the beholder of beauty, while someone else beholds ugliness. Sometimes we are the beauty beheld in other's eyes, and sometimes we are the ugliness beheld in other's eyes. If we try hard enough, we should be able to look past the ugliness that our eyes at first perceive, to find the beauty that lies beneath; the beauty that someone else sees.

It's Only a Good Deal If...

In the summer of 1978 I was a newly married man, starting the second year of my first career, and a first time homeowner. As such, I had plenty of lessons to learn. Here I intend to relate a story and lesson that came to be as a result of home ownership.

I quickly learned that owning a home meant fixing things. There was always something in our home that needed fixed. Things like the toilet running off and on, or a faucet leaking, or a door squeaking, or a loose shelf on the wall, or the cover of an electrical outlet needing replaced. What ever it was, because I did not have my own tools, I frequently had to ask my dad to loan me tools to do the job. Dad was gracious enough to help me out, but sometimes I was slow at returning his tools. This meant that he occasionally had to ask me if I could return one of his tools.

One day he invited me to attend a tool auction with him. It did not occur to me at the time, but as I write this I am certain that he was hoping that I would buy some tools of my own so that he would not have to ask me if he could use his own tools any more. Pretty sneaky!

The auction had all kinds of tools to be bid on. There were power tools such as circular saws and table saws, drills of all sizes and intended uses, tools for specific trades, and hand tools such as hammers and pliers and screwdrivers. Not having either the money, or the need, or know how needed to successfully bid on the power tools, I sat quietly and watched the lively back and forth banter between the auctioneer and the bidders. It was clear, in my opinion, that often time a bidder became overcome with the excitement of the process and bid way to much for an item, just so that he would win the bidding process. It appeared that winning the bid was as important, or even more important, than the worth of the item. The winning bidder always celebrated his victory, sometimes seemingly blind to the fact that he paid too much, or that perhaps he had just purchased something that he did not really need. As I watched and learned, I silently hoped that I would not be one of those bidders, seeking to win the bid rather than to get a good deal.

A set of screwdrivers came up for auction. I began to bid, but dropped out when I felt like the bidding had elevated the price to a point beyond the value. I began to become frustrated, worried that I might have come to a tool auction only to go home empty handed. I mean, if you go to an auction you ought to buy something. Right? About that time, a set of 7 pliers came up for bid. There were several sizes and types of pliers. I began to bid, and stayed with the bidding until I was announced the winner, at a bid of ten dollars. I celebrated just like the other winning bidders had. I had won a bid, and was going home with some tools of my own!

Driving home with my dad, still feeling the joy of victory, I was reveling in my own success. Re-living the event as I drove, I asked, "Seven pairs of pliers for $10, that was a pretty good deal, don't you think". Dad replied, "It is only a good deal if you needed 7 pairs of pliers." The word "need" really hit me hard. The balloon of my jubilation just burst! One pair of pliers, or maybe 2 pair was really all I needed. I did not need 3 sizes of regular pliers. Nor did I need 2 sizes of needle nose pliers, or 2 sizes of wire cutting pliers.

The difference between wanting something and needing something seems such a simple concept. In reality, however, we all struggle with this in our daily lives, and it is not easy to buy out of need rather than want. In fact, I had learned this lesson several years earlier, once again from my father. The fact that I had to be reminded of the difference between need and want simply goes to illustrate how difficult it can be in practice.

About 4 years before attending the tool auction, I was in college at the University of Minnesota, and was taking some rather mathematically intensive chemistry and physics courses. I used an instrument called a slide rule to make the calculations. Most people today do not even know what a slide rule is, but it is very useful for multiplication, division, trigonometry functions, squares, and square root calculations. The hand held calculator was just becoming popular, and was quite expensive, about $150 for a calculator. Our professors recognized that not all students had a calculator, so they would not allow its use on tests. However, the use of a slide rule was permitted on tests.

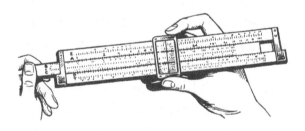

Above: A typical slide rule

As is common with new technology, the price of the hand held calculators began to come down. First to $135, and then miraculously (I thought), down to $105. I called my dad and asked him if he would send me money to buy a calculator, saying, "they will never be cheaper than this!" Looking back, that statement alone is laughable. Today, a similar calculator can be purchased for under $15. Anyway, my dad asked me if I was required to have a calculator for any of my classes. I answered, "no, and in fact we are not allowed to use them on the tests." In my dad's wisdom, he said no. But he did offer to send me money to buy a new slide rule if I needed one.

Dad realized that I did not need a calculator. Rather, I only wanted one. He was right. I wanted to be like the students walking around campus with their calculator hanging from their belt in a pouch. Yes, I was a nerd, and I wanted to look like a nerd! I graduated with my Bachelors Degree in spite of not owning a calculator. I did just fine with my slide rule. I wish I still had it.

I still battle with recognizing need versus want. My house is full of things that I wanted but did not need. This is one of our human weaknesses. Part of the struggle, and indeed part of the means to victory in the struggle, is simply to recognize that there is a distinction between needs and wants. That recognition alone will not prevent me from making decisions based on wants instead of needs, but it is a step in the right direction. Every time that I stop to ask myself, "do I need this, or simply want it?", I am one step closer to victory in the battle. I may loose a skirmish now and then, but the battle continues on. Remember that no matter the cost, it is only a good deal if you needed it.

Regrets

I have done plenty of things in my life that I regret doing. I do not intend to go through a complete list, even if it were possible, of those things. Trust me when I say, there are a lot of things I wish I had not done. Many are mistakes that were made simply as a part of growing up. I spoke earlier about the time I spent learning to curse, and the culmination of that unseemly behavior. That is one of the things in my life that I regret. I learned from that period of life, and I moved on. Such is also true of other actions in my life. However, through learning and moving on, and with the gift of forgiveness in the Sacrament of Reconciliation, I live without being haunted by these regrets. I cannot say the same, however, about regrets that have been caused not by my actions, but rather by my inaction.

The regret that haunts me even to this day, the regret that I wish I could go back in time to rectify, is due to something that I did not do. It was not a sinful action, or a sinful failure to act; thus it does not lend itself to Reconciliation. It is something that I have to live with, and try my best to accept.

In 1917, my grandfather Charles Kissling left his father's farm at the age of 25 and joined the US Army to go fight in World War I. He was sent to France with the Army Infantry in 1918. His unit marched all the way across France, about 350 miles, to the trenches along the France-Germany border. He spent a month in a field hospital in France, but his letters home never tell why he was in the hospital. My dad, grandpa's son, thought that grandpa had some form of pneumonia. It is very likely that grandpa was exposed to some of the poisonous gasses that Germany was using during the War, and had lung damage as a result.

At about the same time, my grandfather Charles Euwer joined the Army at age 18 after graduating from High School in Topeka, Kansas. I do not know anything about his time in the Army during World War I except that he was in the Infantry and in France.

In 1944, the United States was involved in World War II on two fronts; Europe and the Pacific. My father, Ira Charles Kissling, joined the Navy immediately after graduating from High School. He was an only child, and the national policy at the time was that any sole surviving son was not expected to join the military. Yet, he joined anyway, leaving his mother and father to manage the farm without him. Imagine how hard that was for his parents, seeing their only child enlist during a time of war. He was assigned to the USS Hickox (DD673), a Destroyer in the Pacific Ocean, where he served as a SONAR operator. More than 65 years later, when I built him a scale model of the ship he had been on, he pointed to a door on the model and said, "Right there, that is the door I went through when we were called to battle stations."

My mother, Mary Edith Euwer, joined the WACS (Women's Auxiliary Corps) after graduating from High School in 1944. She served as a Switch Board Operator at the Goodyear manufacturing plant in Topeka. Her two older brothers, Charles Jr. and Harold, had already joined the military to help fight the War. Harold joined the Navy, and Charles joined the Army Air Corp (the Air Force as we know it today did not exist during WWII).

Her brother Charles was killed in action just weeks after mom had graduated from High School. He was the Navigator aboard a US B24 Bomber in the 392nd Bomber Group flying out of England. The planes crewmembers were mostly from Kansas (in fact the airport in Eureka is named after the planes Captain, William Milliken). The official name of the plane was the "Model-T", however Charles had informed his family that the crew was in the process of changing the name to "Jayhawker". The plane was lost in combat before the name change could be finalized. The crew was flying their first mission, over Northeast Germany, in the early morning of July 7, 1944. The plane came under heavy attack, described by the 579th Squadron Commander Myron Keilman as "massive fighter attacks and accurate AA". Four aircraft from the 579th Sqdn. were lost that morning. My Uncle's plane went down 2 kilometers South of Egeln, Germany (about 26 K Southwest of Magdeburg, Germany). The local towns people recovered the bodies from the crash scene, identified them, buried them in their town cemetery, and kept written records of the burials. Following the war, the US sent grave recovery teams to recover American Service Personnel lost in the war. Uncle Charles' body was recovered from Egeln, and was re-buried in the Ardennes American Cemetery located in Belgium. I am the only member of his family to have visited his gravesite. It is a beautiful cemetery, and is the final resting place of 5,317 American Service Personnel.

In January 2004, my oldest son Charlie joined the Marine Corps. He stated that "he had been called to be a Marine", and that his "life thus far had been ordered to making him a Marine", and that he "needs to do his part for the US in the Iraq War". In 2006, with a 6 month old daughter and a pregnant wife at home, he was sent to Fallujah, Iraq with the 2nd Marine Division, 2nd Tank Battalion, Charlie Co.

He returned home safely to his wife and 2 daughters.

In March of 1971, I turned 18 years old. Our Country was heavily involved in the Viet Nam War. As is true today, 18-year-old men in the United States must register with Selective Service. At the time I turned 18, we called it registering for the draft. Every month, young men were receiving letters in the mail informing them that they had been selected for the draft, meaning that they were being ordered into the U.S. Military.

On my 18th birthday, my mother picked me up from school and drove me to the Selective Service office in down town St. Paul, Minnesota. There I registered for the draft. I had not given much thought to the possibility of being drafted. I was thinking of which college I would attend. Just as I did not wonder about the potential cost of college, I did not think about the potential of being drafted. At that age I still did not think about consequences a lot, and just like most young people I though I was immortal. Not that immortality entered into my thinking at the time, but that failure to recognize one's own mortality is a symptom of failure to recognize, contemplate, and accept the nature of things yet to come. So, I filled out the registration form, and got back into the car with mom for the drive home.

As we were driving home, mom said very matter of factly, and without any prior discussion, "If you are drafted, I want you to go to Canada." No discussion followed, nor was any discussion necessary. It was very clear to me what she meant. She did not want me to go into the Military, and if I were drafted she wanted me to evade the draft by moving to Canada. You must understand that a draftee failing to report for duty would have a warrant issued for his arrest. By moving to Canada to avoid reporting for duty, would mean never being able to return to the United States without facing the risk of arrest. My mother felt so strongly that she did not want me to go into the Military that she would rather see me move to Canada and never be able to return home. This strong sentiment was not the result of a resistance to the Viet Nam War. Many draft evaders (draft dodgers) did so as a protest to the U.S. involvement in Viet Nam. This was not so with my mom. She did not want to face the possibility of losing a son to war. She had already lost a brother to war, and did not want to lose a son to war.

At that time, I had not given any thought to the Viet Nam War. It was in the news every day. The evening news always had the "body count" of the day: how many American soldiers were killed that day, how many were wounded, how many enemy soldiers were killed, and how many were wounded. The war was unpopular, that was clear. There were frequently protests against the war. And yet, I had failed to form an opinion about the war. The war existed, plain and simple. And I was in high school, getting ready to graduate and go to college. It did not seem to me that I needed to have an opinion about the war. It did not occur to me that perhaps, as a citizen living in a free country, I might have a duty to my country to help stop the spread of a governmental system that was inherently anti-freedom. It did not occur to me that freedom is not free, and that freedom must be protected and fought for. It did not come to mind that perhaps, just perhaps, the people of South Viet Nam wanted the same freedom that I enjoyed and might need my help in obtaining it. No, none of those thoughts entered my mind because I was either incapable of or simply refused to look beyond myself. I thought only of me. I did go to a "Dump the War Rally" in Minneapolis, but only because of the musicians who would be performing there, not because of any animus towards the war. John Denver and Peter Yarrow (of Peter, Paul, and Mary) performed at that rally. Also, it was free to attend.

I came to decide that I would not join or allow myself to be drafted into the Military. So,

I developed the attitude that if I was drafted, I would do just as my mother wanted me to do. I would go to Canada as a draft dodger. Yes, I would go to Canada in order to spare her the possibility of losing a son to war, not so much because I had developed any tangible opposition to the war itself. Also, I thought I would go to Canada simply out of a selfish thought that serving in the Military would get in the way of what I wanted to do. As I look back, I am amazed that it did not enter my mind that leaving the United States and fleeing to Canada would also get in the way of what I wanted to do. I think that just illustrates how indifferent I was to anything beyond myself.

As it would turn out, I was never drafted. I never had to actually make a decision that would require action on my part. Now I must live with the reality that I never served my country in the Military. I broke the chain of Service that was started by my grandfathers, continued by my father and mother, my uncles, (one of whom, as Abraham Lincoln said, "gave his last full measure of devotion", and then re-formed by my son. The cause for my regret is obvious: both of my grandfathers answered their country's call in WWI, my mother and father and my two only uncles answered the call in WWII, and my son answered the call during the Iraq War. I however, did not answer the call. When my country needed me, when my fellow Americans were fighting and dying in Viet Nam I turned my back. I yielded to my mom's fear of losing another family member to war, and to my own indifference. I now regret that I did not serve. I am not sure when I first felt the sting of regret from my inaction, but it became very palpable when my oldest son announced that he "had been called to be a Marine" shortly after the Iraq War had begun. Now I am left with the realization that my son did something that I should have done.

This regret is something that I cannot undo or rectify. So I live with it, always with me. Sometimes bubbling just below the surface, sometimes boiling over. I can rationalize that everything has worked out for the best, and that it was God's plan for my life. If I had joined the military after high school, I am sure that my life would have developed much differently. I know for sure that not joining probably kept two bad things from happening. First, my girlfriend at the time (who broke up with me, for another guy, after my first year of college) would possibly have committed the dastardly deed of sending me a Dear John letter. Secondly, my mom did not lose a son to war.

Looking at my life today, my wonderful wife and children, my daughter in laws, my grandchildren, and the profession I practiced for 34 very satisfying years, I can say that I would not change a thing. This creates a bit of contradiction, doesn't it? On the one hand, I wish I could go back in time and change my decision and attitude, and join the military to serve my country; but on the other hand I would not change a thing about my life. Such is the reality of my regret and the contradiction it creates, and the challenge of living with it. If only I could go back in time, join the military, and yet have everything else remain unchanged. Of course, that is not possible.

During the course of our lives, we make decisions and choices. A major part of each life is exactly that, making one choice after another. Every one of those decisions and choices that we make has an impact on the rest of our lives. We make those decisions and choices with the information available at the time, and we try to make the best choice based on that information. Then we must live with the effect of each choice. That is the lesson here. We must live our lives moment-by-moment, day-by-day, making decisions and acting in the present. And then we must do our best to live with our decisions and actions, or even our inactions. Some are easier to live with than others. Some will continue to haunt us, but we cannot let them control and dominate us. We must do our best to accept them, and keep moving on. I have learned that if I dwell on such things too long, I actually begin to have a chronic stomach ache. The underlying emotional turmoil begins to physically affect me. I am certain that I am not alone in this affectation, so this lesson is for you too. Don't dwell on the past, whether there be episodes of action or inaction; do your best to live with them and learn from them. As George Santayana wrote, "Those who cannot remember the past are condemned to repeat it." The past is not to be forgotten, but rather as Jesus' Mother Mary did "She kept all these things, pondering them in her heart". So I fight the battle within, pondering my past in my heart, trying not to dwell on it to the point of physical discomfort, and learning from it so as to not repeat my mistakes. Today I try to ask myself, "who if not me, and when if not now?" Imperfect as I am, I still do not always answer the call, whatever it may be. But, I continue to strive. Hoping not to create more regret than I already have.

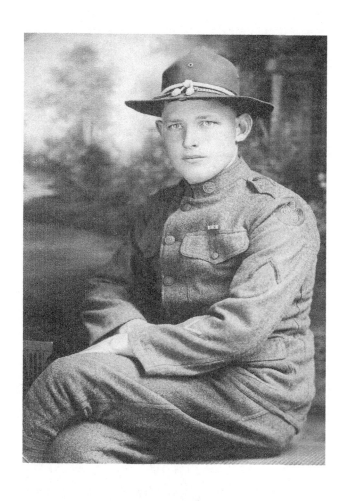

Above: Charles E. Kissling, World War I

Above: Charles T. Euwer, World War I

Above: Ira Charles Kissling, World War II

Above: Mary E. (Euwer) Kissling, World War II

Above: Charles T. Euwer, Jr. and Harold Euwer, World War II

Above: Charles T. Euwer, Jr., World War II

Above: Harold Euwer, World War II

Above: Charles T. Euwer, Jr. (left) with members of his flight crew, taken June 23, 1944.

Above: Air Crew of the "Model-T" which was to be renamed the "Jayhawk". Charles Euwer is second row, third from left.

Above: The "Service Flag" which hung in the window of the Euwer family home during WWII. Originally, two blue stars, one for Charles and one for Harold. Notice the gold star, which my mom sewed over the original blue star when Charles was killed in action.

Above: Charles L. Kissling, Iraq War

Above: Charles L. Kissling saying goodbye before leaving for Iraq.
Below: Charles L Kissling preparing for a mission as machine gunner on top of the lead vehicle in Fallujah, Iraq.

Don't Put Powder on the Baby!

As a new father, I was anxious to perform some fatherly duties. You know, like changing a diaper. My wife was now in her room, recovering from the deliver of our first-born and the surgery immediately following delivery because of childbirth complications. Our baby was in the room with her a few hours daily as his head was gradually reshaping into a normal shape. The other hours, he was in the hospital nursery. With both mom and son recovering from the difficult delivery, we did not get to spend much time with the baby until 48 hours after birth.

The hospital had given us a "new parents" bag of helpful items. Included in the bag were things such as disposable diapers, baby wipes, baby shampoo, baby oil, and baby powder. If you have ever had the experience of having a loved one in the hospital and spent much time with them, you know that there can be a lot of boredom. Fighting off some of this boredom, I actually opened the goody bag and perused the contents. It seemed to me that everything I might need to successfully change my new son's diaper was at my fingertips. I could hardly wait for a chance to put myself to the test. I was hoping to show that I could be a good father and husband, and help with some of the tasks of raising a baby; especially the task of changing a diaper.

Each time the baby was in the room with us, I dutifully checked his diaper hoping to find a diaper that needed to be changed. Unfortunately, the nurses usually put a new diaper on him just prior to bringing him to our room. On our third, and last day, in the hospital I finally got my chance. Upon checking his diaper, I found a small dab of black, tarry excrement. I could hardly contain my joy! This was my chance to prove myself. My chance to prove that I had what it takes to be a daddy.

So, I began the process. I washed my hands extra well, lots of soap and lots of rinsing. Then I prepared a proper work area, arranging the necessary items in an efficient manner. I felt it important to do this right the first time, and to make a good impression. Each item was placed within easy reach so that I would not have to walk away from the baby during the process. I went through the process silently in my head several times just to be sure I was ready. I undid the tape fasteners of my three-day-old son's dirty diaper. Then I lifted his legs and removed the diaper, leaving it open and setting it off to the side. Using a baby wipe, I meticulously cleaned his bottom, being careful to not rub too hard, yet hard enough to be sure that I did not leave behind any trace of poop. I placed the used wipes into the dirty diaper, then grabbed a new diaper and opened it and placed it beneath my son. I then picked up the container of baby powder, and liberally applied it to my son's bottom, spreading it out so as to fully cover his skin. Next, I carefully closed the diaper over him, and sealed the tape fasteners in place. Standing back and looking at my handiwork, I was truly proud. I, of course, could not see myself, but I would bet that I was wearing a smile of tremendous proportions. There it was, my first diaper change. I had proved to myself, to my wife, and to my son that I could at least perform this one duty of fatherhood.

Soon after my successful demonstration of diaper changing competence, a nurse came in to check on us and on the baby. Without saying anything, she opened his diaper to see if it needed changed. Then she said, "Who changed the baby's diaper?" I could hardly contain my pride and blurted out "I did!" She replied curtly, saying "Don't put powder on the baby! It gunks up his crack." She proceeded to wipe away the powder remnants, and replaced the diaper with a new one.

I was devastated. I had felt so proud of what I had done, and then the nurse burst my bubble and cut me down to size. I went from feeling so high to feeling so depressed. I thought I had done a thorough job, using the items that had been provided in our "new parent's" bag. If I was not supposed to use the baby powder, why was it in the bag? I convinced myself that this nurse simply did not know what she was talking about. Perhaps she did not know that the hospital provided baby powder to new parents, and therefore the hospital implicitly was telling new parents that it was acceptable to use powder on the baby. Right or wrong, I brushed off her admonishment, and determined that I would continue to use powder when I changed a diaper; but perhaps not until we were at home.

Since that time, I have changed a lot of diapers. I have learned that baby boys will pee in my face while I lean over them if I don't cover them quickly after removing their diaper. That was a big surprise the first time it happened, a really big surprise! Not that I am a slow learner, but yes, it happened more than once. I am not too proud to admit that each of my three sons managed to pee in my face. Perhaps each was simply preparing me for the terrible two's, or for later years when they would challenge me in other ways; ways more significant than a little, or a lot, of pee in the face. I continued to like to use baby powder when changing diapers, although not every time. I still have that first bottle of baby powder, and I cherish it. When I look at it and hold it in my hands, I am instantly taken back in time to that first diaper change, and that first lesson in proper diaper changing technique. And it still brings a smile to my face.

Once You Have Children, Everything Changes

In the late Spring and early Summer of 1992, our family included 3 sons, aged 9 years, 5 years, and 5 months. We led busy lives that revolved around our children. There was school, pre-school, infant care, after school activities, soccer, and baseball. Sleep was a treasured commodity, and when not awakened by a crying or hungry infant, was at best shallow sleep. So, one night, when the tornado sirens sounded at 3AM I was jolted awake immediately and sprang into action instinctively.

There was a time, before children, when the tornado sirens would arouse a sense of excitement deep within me. As a lover of science, I found tornados to be extremely interesting. They are such a focused source of enormous power. The conic shape of a tornado is a beautiful thing to behold. Yes, tornados can be very destructive when they encounter trees and man made structures. Perhaps it is that contradiction of beauty and destructiveness that makes the tornado so fascinating. So when the sirens would sound, alerting the local population to the presence of a tornado, I would instantly go on tornado look out. This is in direct opposition to what we are told to do when the sirens sound. We are told to take shelter, preferably in a location below ground such as a basement. It is highly discouraged to go outside and watch for the tornado, but yet that is exactly what I would do, before children. When the sirens sounded, I would go outside and scan the skies for the tornado itself, or for the telltale signs of a tornado such as swirling clouds. If rain or hale, both common occurrences in tornado weather, was too severe then I would seek shelter under the porch or in such a place as to keep me out of the weather while still allowing a good view of the sky. Ah, but that was all before children came into my life.

So on that particular night, when the tornado sirens sounded at 3AM and I sprang into action, it was not to go outside to scan the skies. No. I sprang into action to protect our children. I must have been sleeping well, because I awoke with a startle and jumped out of bed. I told my wife to grab the baby and get downstairs, then I ran into the two older boys room to awaken them. I did not even take time to put on my glasses, which meant that I could see virtually nothing with clarity. I woke the 9 year old and told him to go directly to the basement. Then I grabbed the still sleeping 5-year old into my arms and ran toward the stairwell. Without slowing down, I turned to go down the stairs, and in my blurry haste missed the first step with my foot. My arms were full, carrying a sleeping boy. My vision was blurred since I had not put on my glasses. Having missed the first step, I then missed the second step as well. My lead foot was now sliding from step to step, and my trail foot remained behind me at the top of the stairs. I could not let go of my son, so I was not able to reach out to grab the stair rail. Thus, I began to bounce down the stairs, trying my best to avoid a head first tumble, and trying to protect the boy in my arms. In the blink of an eye I landed at the bottom of the stairs on my back. One of my legs was sprawled out to my side, and the other leg was trapped painfully beneath me. I was certain that the leg beneath me was broken. My son was now sitting upright on my chest, asking me "Daddy, why did you wake me up?" Meanwhile my wife was still gathering the baby and necessary items such as pillows and blankets. She heard the commotion and noise created by the sound of my uncontrolled descent down the stairs and the thud of my landing. She knew that I had headed for the stairs carrying our middle son. I heard her call out, "Is Clint all right?" That's right, she did not ask, "Are you all right?" I was lying in pain at the bottom of the stairs, with what I was certain was a broken leg twisted beneath me, and a young son sitting on my chest wanting to know why I woke him, and my wife wanted to know if our son was all right. I weakly responded, "He's fine."

The episode that night was a sudden reminder of how much my life had changed since having children. No longer was I outside watching for tornados in the storm. Now my interest was in the protection of my family. I had sacrificed my own interests for the safety of my family. In addition to this, I was no longer the most important person in my wife's life. Now, I shared that importance with my sons, and rightfully so. When she asked if our son was all right, she was not ignoring me, but was rather acknowledging the fact that our boys were reliant on us; that the boy in my arms was reliant on me for a safe trip to the basement.

Yes, when children enter our lives, many things change. Our interests change to match the interests of our children. Our actions change so as to facilitate the safety of our children. Our spouse, instead of being the most important person in our life, shares that distinction with the children as the most important people in our life.

As much as I used to enjoy watching for a tornado, I discovered that I was even more fulfilled by caring for my children. That seems like a fair trade to me.

Success or Failure? A Matter of Perspective

When my middle son, Clint, was in Webelos Scouts, I was his den leader. Webelos is for boys who are in Cub Scouts, and are in the 4th or 5th grade. It is the bridge between Cub Scouts and Boy Scouts. The boys gain an early and minimal exposure to Boys Scouts activities and ideals. They may experience their first overnight camping, generally with their parent and the other members of the den. In the summer between 4th and 5th grade, our Webelos den went to camp Tawakoni for a two night camping trip. The boys, accompanied by a parent, were able to shoot BB guns, bow and arrows, and group games, as well as spend two nights sleeping on the ground in a tent.

When I was a boy, my dad bought a large Coleman canvas tent for family outings. The tent was 10 feet by 13 feet, and tall enough to stand in. I remember camping and sleeping in that tent with our family, and enjoying every minute of that time. One memory that stands out is of a camping trip to Lake Murray in southern Oklahoma. A tremendous thunderstorm blew in, accompanied by lots of lightning. The flashes of lightning and the rumble of thunder terrified my little sister. I tried to comfort her by explaining the scientific wonder of lightning, and how each bolt contained such a massive amount of electricity. Why I thought that information would serve to comfort her rather than scare the wits out of her, I do not know. Either way, she seemed to be calmed by my explanation.

When my sons were quite young, we went camping in that same tent. That tent had been through storms and high winds and kept us dry through all during my youth, and now it had the chance to do the same for my young family. It performed flawlessly during a hard thunderstorm in the Ozarks when our first two boys were too young to remember. I had used it for my oldest son's Webelos camp outs, and now I wanted to use that nearly 35-year-old tent again for Clint's Webelos camping. I wanted him, and his fellow Webelos, to have the same great camping experiences that I had, and the same great camping memories that I have.

We arrived at Camp Tawakoni early in the evening and began setting up the tent. The boys worked at stretching the tent out on the ground, and doing their best to hammer in the stakes. I helped them assemble the tent poles, put them in place, and then raise the tent. Immediately, the boys unzipped the doors and began running into and through the tent with the joy and energy that only a boy can possess. It was wonderful watching them enjoy the tent that was now theirs for 3 days. I persuaded the boys to begin moving their personal gear, clothing and sleeping bags into the tent. As they performed that task, I sat up my own small, 2-man tent. I positioned it directly facing the boy's tent so that I would have quick access to them if needed. I knew from experience, that the first night would be especially hard to get the boys settled down and quiet so they could sleep. I also knew that if they did not sleep, neither would I, or any of the other parents who were camping with us in their own near-by tents. So, my tent was in a position such that I could easily hear the boys, and they could easily hear me telling them to be quiet. The other parents set up tents in the same general vicinity, but certainly not as close as my tent.

That evening, I herded the boys into their tent at bed time, advising them to get some sleep because tomorrow would be a busy day, and I lead them in their night prayer. Thirty minutes later, it was necessary to quiet them down, as their talking had gradually gone from quiet whispers to outright talking to full-blown laughter and games. The noise cycle repeated itself again, but after a second admonition they remained quiet and were fast asleep. Soon, so was I.

Sometime during the night, a storm moved in. I really do not have a good sense of what time, other than it was probably about 3AM. It began with distant thunder, and quickly grew to high winds, heavy rain, and nearby cloud to ground lightning. Suddenly, through the noise of the storm, I began to hear the boys yelling. Looking out of my tent in the darkness, the lightning illuminated the boys standing in the rain where the tent was supposed to be. I quickly jumped out of my tent, and discovered that the large tent the boys had been sleeping in had collapsed to the ground. When the boys and I tried to re-raise the tent, we discovered that one of the main tent poles had broken.

I quickly began to help the water soaked boys into the nearby tents of the other parents, and guided my own son into my tent. Then, with the storm still in good force, I grabbed every piece of dry clothing and towels that I had (as the den leader I had learned to bring plenty of extra clothing and extra towels), and ran back out of my tent into the storm to deliver something dry to each of the boys who were now scattered in several tents. Then I, soaked to the bone and cold from the wetness, climbed back into my tent to join my son. Together, we opened my sleeping bag to serve as a blanket for us, and tried to get warm again.

Perhaps 15 minutes later, I heard someone yelling, "where's _____"? I called back into the dark, "isn't he in the tent with you?" The answer came back, "no!" I stepped back out into the storm and went to several tents asking, "is _____ in there with you?" The occupants of each tent responded that he was not in that tent. I began to fear that he might still be in the collapsed tent.

I ran through the storm to the tent now laying flat on the ground with water puddled on its surface. Getting down on my hands and knees, I found the collapsed doorway. I was immediately surprised by the sheer weight of the wet canvas as I tried to lift the door flap so that I could crawl in. The weight forced me to the ground on my stomach, and forced me to "army crawl" into the tent. I discovered that the bathtub style floor of the tent was now holding 2-3 inches of water within its confines. The weight of the wet canvas prevented me from being able to raise myself up to my hands and knees. I was barely able to lift my head enough to keep my face out of the pool of water that the tent now held. Suddenly, the reality of the situation hit me like a bolt of lightning. If there was a boy trapped in this collapsed tent, he could drown, and the amount of time that had passed meant that he likely already had drowned. I felt a surge of adrenalin and fear race through my body, and a new sense of urgency, which grew into panic. I began to stretch my arms forward as far as they could reach, and wiggle my flat body along the floor of the tent with the tent roof weighing heavily on my back. I reached and pulled as fast as I could. I could only feel water logged sleeping bags and the boys possessions scattered everywhere I reached. I struggled to reach every corner of the tent, fighting against the items in the tent, the weight of the tent on my back, and the pooled water. I was full of fear that I would feel an arm or a leg somewhere in that dark, water filled world that was once a shelter for the boys. After what seemed like an eternity, but was probably only minutes, in that flattened tent, I came to the conclusion that a boy was not trapped in that collapsed tent. I felt a bit of relief, but the question still remained: where was he?

Leaving the tent, getting back to my feet, I once again began to go from tent to tent. This time I did not limit my search to the few tents in the immediate vicinity of my own tent. Finally, five or six tents down the row, I found the missing boy. He had wandered on his own down the row of tents and just climbed into one, surprising its occupants. With the mystery now solved, I let everyone know that I had found him and that he was safe. Returning to my tent, wet and wide awake in the middle of the night, I tried to get dry and go back to sleep.

When dawn began to break, I was the first person out of any of the tents. I surveyed the area, and could see that my old canvas tent was the only casualty of the storm. One of the main upright, spring-loaded poles had snapped. That tent had been through storms like this before, and escaped unscathed. Whether this storm was worse, or perhaps just the age of the tent led to its demise. I do not know. I was broken hearted looking at that tent in a crumpled, flattened, water soaked mess on the ground. The boys were all up and about by then, and I sent them up to the dining hall for breakfast. Because we still had another night of camping, I began to work on trying to resurrect my old friend. I was able to "jury-rig" a pole to replace the broken upright, and got the tent standing again. It was obvious to me that the next night would likely be the last camping trip for my beloved tent. I pulled all of the water logged sleeping bags out of the tent, and tried to wring out as much water from them as I could, then spread them out on the ground. Next, I was able to remove all of the bits of clothing and other belongings that remained in the tent. Finally, I drained the bathtub floor, emptying the water that still remained within the tent. What a disaster this had been.

I was devastated, and felt that I had let the boys down on what, for some of them, was their first real camping experience. A traumatic experience like this, at an early age, could very well cause a young person to leave scouting and never want to go camping again. If that were to happen, I would hold myself responsible. I felt terrible. After breakfast, one of the parents volunteered to take the wet sleeping bags into town to a laundry-mat where the bags could be dried out. We went through the morning activities, the boys seeming no worse for the wear, and I continuing to feel like a failure. Sometime later that day, one of the boys approached me and said, "Mr. Kissling, that was fun last night. The worst thing that happens when my family goes camping is that the trailer shakes a little!"

Here I was, feeling sorry for myself, feeling like a failure, feeling like I had let the boys down, and feeling let down by the tent of my youthful memories. Then, at the depth of my despair, a young boy told me that he had fun; telling me that what I saw as a disaster, he saw as fun. Fun that could perhaps carry with it the meaning of success, at least in the context that this boy was enjoying this unique camping experience. From my perspective, the outing was a disaster. However, from this boy's perspective, the outing was "fun".

I think that we all have experiences like this. Something that we see as a disaster or a failure turns into a success when viewed from a different perspective. Sometimes we should look at life through another set of eyes; a set of eyes other than our own. Things are not always as they seem from first glance, or from one's own perspective. Trying to find a different perspective may very well produce a different picture. Wallowing in my own self-pity, I was unable to see the happenings of that night as anything but failure on my part, and on the part of my childhood tent. It was only when a young boy opened my eyes to the event as he saw it that I was able to see some positive come out of this camping trip.

Yes, that was the last outing for the tent my dad had purchased some 35 years earlier. The tent that had been the source of so many good memories for me, had now given those boys a memory that could last a lifetime, just as it had done for me. That hardly sounds like a failure to me. I only had to see it from a different perspective.

When God Speaks

In the Fall of 1998 I offered to help the coaching staff of the Bishop Carroll High School boys soccer team. My intention was to do exactly that, simply help. However, in high school athletics, there is no mechanism that allows a person to simply help. Thus, I became a member of the coaching staff, and was made coach of the "C" team. This was more than I had bargained for.

In the first week we held 2 practices daily, the first practice starting in the early morning darkness. The team members started the morning with a warm up run. After the run, each coach spent a few minutes talking to one of the four classes (freshman, sophomore, junior, senior). Each day, the coaches rotated as to which class each would address. On the third morning I was assigned to address the seniors after they finished their warm up run.

I felt completely unprepared and inadequate to speak to the seniors. They already had three years of experience playing high school soccer, and they were the leaders of the team as a whole. Who was I to address these young men? I had no previous experience coaching at this level, and it was only my third day, yet I was expected to address these players and deliver a motivational talk. I had no idea what to say to them. As they finished the warm up run, a voice in my head, or perhaps even just words in my head, said to me "tell them that the first shall be last and the last shall be first, and how that applies to being a leader."

So that is what I did. I reminded them that the Bible says, "the first shall be last and the last shall be first". Then I told them that as seniors they were expected to be leaders on the team, and that a good leader puts himself last. A good leader puts the interests and needs of those beneath him above his own interests and needs. A good leader sacrifices by being the first to practice every day, and the last to leave. A good leader does not simply tell someone what to do; he helps them and leads them in doing it until they are able to do it on their own.

That evening, the team had a team Mass at Christ the King Catholic Church in Wichita. The Gospel reading was from the twentieth chapter of Matthew. That particular Gospel reading tells the story of a vineyard owner hiring workers throughout the day. At the end of the day, the owner paid each worker the full days wage, regardless of whether the worker had worked the full day or not. The story ends with the statement "Thus, the last will be first, and the first will be last". The Priest's Homily, immediately after the Gospel reading, focused on the last statement of the Gospel reading. He explained to the team how that statement applies to them in the context of being team members, and especially being leaders on the team.

I sat in my seat quivering from the realization of what had occurred that day. After the Mass, one of the team members I had addressed early in the morning came to me saying, "you set that up, didn't you Coach?" I assured him that I had not set it up.

Some would say that what happened that day was simply a coincidence, which didn't really mean anything special. I, however, am convinced that the voice of God spoke to me that morning. No, I did not recognize it at the time it happened. In fact, I did not entertain the possibility that I had in fact received Divine guidance until I heard the Gospel reading at the evening Mass. Hearing the Priest deliver the same message to the team that I had delivered in the morning only served to confirm my suspicion. At that point, it was obvious to me that I received Divine guidance in the form of the Voice of God speaking into my ears.

I suspect that I, and perhaps everyone, hear the Voice of God at various times within our lives. However, most of the time we do not realize it at the time. Perhaps, most of the time we never realize that God has spoken to us. There are many ways to explain away the voice;

such as, it was my own idea, or it was just a coincidence. I think we only need to be open to the possibility that God speaks to us. If we accept that possibility, then we are able to recognize the times in our lives when He has spoken to us. It would be much easier if God would announce Himself like he did in the movie <u>Oh God</u>, which starred George Burns as God, and John Denver as the person being spoken to by God. The reality, however, is that He does not announce Himself, or introduce Himself, when he speaks. If he did, we most likely would follow His guidance as if it were an order. But remember, God gave us free will. He wants us to do His will by free choice, not because He introduced Himself and told us what to do. If we simply allow for the possibility that he speaks to us without introduction, we can begin to see the times in our past when He did indeed speak. It would be easier if we had immediate recognition of His Voice, but we don't. I don't think He wants it to be easy. He wants us to choose to know, love, and serve Him by our own free willed choice. Not by force.

Make yourself open to the possibility of guidance from God, and you will begin to recognize those times in your life when He was there guiding you, and perhaps speaking to you.

As if recognizing the times when God speaks to you is not challenging enough, understanding the message is yet another challenge. As it says in the Old Testament Book of Isaiah (55:8), "For my thoughts are not your thoughts, and your ways are not my ways, says the Lord."

In the summer of 2003, I heard a voice during the night saying, "I am talking to Charlie". Charlie is my oldest son. He had just finished two years of relatively unproductive college, much as were my first years of college. He had started at one college, playing soccer and as he said, "not taking any courses that I like". He transferred to another college for the next semester. It was obvious to me that he was searching for direction in his life. During the summer school break, he became a teacher in the Totus Tuus Program for a Diocese in Colorado. He traveled from one Parish to another along with 3 other Totus Tuus team members presenting one-week programs for school age children, teaching them about the Catholic Faith. The team members were also charged with daily group and individual prayer, seeking guidance for their futures and vocation in life.

So when I received the message, "I am talking to Charlie", I knew that God was telling me that he was guiding my son. I interpreted this to mean that he was leading my son to the Priesthood in the Catholic Church. Of this I was certain.

Upon arriving home at the end of the summer, Charlie asked to speak to my wife and I after dinner. When we set down he said, "Mom and dad, I have a calling." I remained silent, as a father should when his son is about to proclaim his life's calling, but I said to my self, "I knew that! God gave me a head's up. You are being called to be a Priest." Then Charlie proclaimed, "I have been called to be a United States Marine." Wait! What? My mind whirled in unexpected confusion. I flashed back to the time when he was 12 years old and watching the Cadets march at the Air Force Academy. I had asked him what he would think about going to college there. He had replied, "I don't know dad, that looks awfully disciplined." My young son telling me that the Air Force Academy looked "awfully disciplined", and now eight years later he wants to be a Marine? Talk about discipline! Charlie went on to explain, "My whole life thus far has been ordered towards making me into a Marine. Scouts, sports, all were preparing me to be a Marine."

Soon after, he joined the Marine Corps and served active duty for five years with a tour of duty in Fallujah, Iraq where he led men in combat. Indeed, his life coupled with Marine

Corps training, had led him to being a Marine. A good Marine at that. One of his fellow Marines once said to me, "Sir, I want you to know that I trust your son with my life".

God had given him the necessary gifts and talents to be a Marine, and God led him to that end. God's plan for him was not my plan. God's ways are not our ways. God knew the gifts he had given Charlie, and He knew how Charlie had developed those gifts as he grew to adulthood. That summer, God spoke to me but I did not understand His full meaning, His full plan. He also spoke to my son, Charlie. Whether Charlie heard a physical voice as I had, I do not know. Perhaps he simply heard the words in his head, in much the same manner as had occurred to me several years before. Either way, Charlie got the message.

The lessons here are two-fold. First, be open to God speaking to you. Recognize that He does speak to us. You may not hear Him in an outright physical full-throated voice. You may only hear a whisper, or simply words in your head. Maybe even just a nudge of guidance. Be prepared to not immediately realize that the voice you heard, or the words in your head were God speaking to you. It may take minutes, hours, days, weeks, or even years before you realize that message to have been the voice of God. You may never come to that realization.

But, if you are open to Him, and if you look back in your life you just may find times when He has indeed spoken to you.

Secondly, don't be surprised if you do not fully understand His message, or if you misinterpret His meaning. His thoughts are not our thoughts. Give yourself time to process the message, continue your conversation with God. Eventually, the meaning of his message will be made clear. Perhaps not until we see Him face to face; but certainly then if not before.

On Sharing Suffering

When I was a boy, I had a chance to go to Philmont Scout Ranch, but I let the fear of failure keep me from going. As an adult leader in my son's Boy Scout troop I was given another opportunity to go to Philmont, this time as a leader with a crew that my son was in. I jumped at the chance to make up for what I felt was one of the mistakes made in my youth.

The reality is, however, that a trek at Philmont is an easier task for a 14-18 year old boy than for a 47 year old, out of shape man. Yes, that was me. Not terribly out of shape, but with my weight approaching 200 pounds, I was 50 pounds heavier than when I left high school, and nearly 20 pounds heavier than I should have been. Added to that, I carried more weight in my pack than I really needed to, all with the goal of comfort after a long day of hiking. I carried a tripod stool to sit on, so I would not have to sit on the ground, or on a log or rock. I also carried more clothes than I needed, so that I would be sure to be warm in the cool evenings. In addition to personal gear, each of us carried a share of the crew equipment, such as tents, cooking pots, food, heavy rope for hanging the food out of the reach of bears, stoves and fuel, saw, toilet paper, and shovel.

The first day on the trail was not so bad. I hesitate to say that it was easy, but it was in no way difficult. We only walked about 2-3 miles, and most of that was on relatively flat terrain, only making a short climb as we approached our first night's camping site. I wondered to myself, "what was I so afraid of as a youth, this isn't that hard".

The second day on the trail proved not to be as easy as the first. We hiked about 6 miles, gaining altitude nearly the whole distance. One half mile section was steep, and without switchbacks, meaning that we walked straight up. I began to feel a blister forming on the ball of one foot after that climb. When we reached camp, the boys headed off to do some pole climbing. As for me, I stayed behind nursing a bad headache (most likely from the altitude).

Our third day of hiking was blessedly a shorter distance, but continued our climb in elevation. I was not terribly aware of the blister that started to form the day before, because I was battling what had become a constant headache. Once in camp, and having set up our tents, all I wanted to do was lay down.

Day four of our trek found us leaving camp at daybreak, without taking down our tents and without the weight of our heavy backpacks. We were headed for an all day hike to the top of Mt. Baldy, which peaks at 12,441 feet, and then a return back to our camp. The hike started easy enough with a mild climb, my blister was annoying but not debilitating, and the headache was still a constant companion. At one point, we stopped for a few minutes rest. I remember hearing nothing but the sound of my own heavy breathing, in and out, in and out. When I asked if I was the only person breathing hard, the rest of the group assured me that I was not. Still, I could hear only my own panting, no other. The higher up the mountain we went, the heavier the breathing and the more frequent the need for rest stops. Eventually, beyond the tree line and climbing steadily upwards on loose rocks, I could go only about 100 yards before the need for a stop to catch my breath. The headache was growing worse and worse, and I was trying my best to not let it show. Finally, standing on the mountain peak and taking in the breathtaking view, it all seemed to be worthwhile and I forgot about my blister and headache. Seeing the beauty of God's handiwork from the top of a mountain seemed to have a soothing affect. In my mind, the difficulty of the climb began to be diminished, and I began to think about how nice it would be to make the climb again. By the time we got back to camp, it was time for dinner. The headache was back and all I wanted to do was lay down.

The fifth day of hiking found us carrying our heavy backpacks   again. The blister on the ball of my foot began to feel like a rock in my boot. During one of the rest stops I even removed the boot to be sure that a rock wasn't the cause of the discomfort. The headache was still my constant companion. The worsening of the blister seemed to be the straw that broke the camel's back. My attitude began a downward spiral, and I was no longer able to hide my pain. That evening I had to force myself to eat. My general discomfort was becoming obvious to the rest of the crew. One of the boys said, "Mister Kissling, are you all right?" I simply replied, "No." Suddenly everyone became very quiet, finishing dinner in silence. I drained my blister, took more Tylenol and went to bed early.

The next morning, as we were packing our packs and dividing up the crew gear, the boys voluntarily took my share and divided it among themselves, leaving no crew gear or food for me to carry. They did this without asking me.   As a result of their generous actions, my pack would be significantly lighter. Conversely, each of their packs would be heavier. They had decided as a group to lighten my load, increasing their own loads. They had effectively chosen to reduce my suffering by taking some of it upon themselves. They were each making a personal sacrifice, on my behalf. A sacrifice that I had not asked for, did not deserve, and had not done anything to earn. A sacrifice that they were making freely and willingly; a sacrifice that they chose to make; a sacrifice that they chose to make without any expectation of return. By the end of that day, I was feeling much better, the headache nearly gone, and the blister no longer feeling like a rock in the bottom of my boot. Was the improvement simply a result of the lighter backpack I carried that day? Was the improvement simply a result of my body finally becoming acclimated to the altitude? Or was the improvement the result of other persons freely choosing to make a sacrifice on my behalf? I don't know. What I do know is that my recovery that evening seemed, at the time, to be miraculous.

We are all called to serve each other; to put others needs before our own needs. This sometimes requires sacrifice on our part. One of the most noble acts any person can do is to sacrifice on behalf of another person; especially when that sacrifice is unrequested, and is not expected to be returned. Many men sacrifice daily to provide for their families by going to work at jobs they do not like. They go to work day after day, not because they like the job, but rather simply to provide income for their families. Many women sacrifice daily for their families by cooking, cleaning, and being a taxi service. Sometimes these women have given up a career to stay at home for the family; sometimes these women do all of the family chores and duties while at the same time working at a job or career to help provide income for the family. What parent does not wish to absorb and take into themselves the suffering of sick children? These sacrifices are offered freely, without being asked, and by choice. Such sacrifices are truly examples of putting others needs ahead of our own needs and desires. Such sacrifices follow the model of sacrifice that Jesus offered for us.

I think that sometimes, perhaps most times, it is easier for us to make sacrifice for another than it is for us to let others make sacrifice for us. "The Servant Song" (#387 in *Breaking Bread 2018*), written by Richard Gillard has a line that says, "Pray that I may have the grace to let you be my servant, too." Too often, we find it hard to allow someone else to sacrifice for us, to serve us; especially if that sacrifice would result in suffering on the part of the other. We are reluctant to allow another person to suffer for us, while we willingly suffer and sacrifice for others.   It requires humility to admit that you may need help. We would rather not accept that we need another person's help, especially when it suggests any sense of inadequacy. I was in exactly that position while hiking at Philmont. I was suffering badly, but felt that if I admitted that, I would be declaring myself inadequate and not up to the rigors of the trek. I would have been reinforcing my childhood fears; those fears that I was not strong enough or tough enough to complete a Philmont trek. So I tried to hide my suffering and discomfort as best I could, until I could not hide it any longer. I refused to ask for help. I refused to admit my need for help. I refused to show any humility. It was only in the morning, when I was mentally too broken to resist, that I was able to accept the help of my fellow crewmembers. I did not have the will to fight against the unequal distribution of crew gear that occurred as a result of the boys taking my share of gear for themselves. If they had asked me, I may have tried to argue against them, I do not know. My ego would have said no, but at that moment my will to fight was broken, and I quietly accepted what they were doing. The moment I lifted that pack, now significantly lighter, onto my back, I was grateful for the selfless sacrifice that those boys made. The boys never said so, but I am certain that I was not the only person who benefited from their selfless act. There was no grumbling from them about the extra weight each had taken on. Each of those boys must also have felt a certain sense of pride at carrying more weight. I imagine that each also felt good about the help that they had given me. The Boy Scout motto is "Do a Good Turn Daily". On that day, those boys did a "good turn" for me.

In helping others, we accomplish two purposes. First of course, is the help that we provide. Second, and just as important even though it is seldom recognized, is the good that we do for ourselves. Who doesn't feel good after doing something to help another person? Just as it is important for each of us to put others needs ahead of our own needs, and make sacrifices for others, we must recognize that this also means that others must allow and accept our sacrifice on their behalf. That means that each of us must be willing to not only sacrifice, and suffer if necessary, for others, but we must also be willing to let others sacrifice and suffer for us. Any time we fail to allow another person to help or sacrifice for us, we deny that person the opportunity to do something that makes them feel good, makes them feel useful. Think of that. We must allow others to suffer for us. We must humble ourselves to accept the sacrifice and suffering of others on our behalf. If we are unable to let others serve us, we will be less able to serve others. By the Grace of God, Jesus came to serve us, suffer for us, and gave the ultimate sacrifice of his life for us. That same Grace leads us to serve, sacrifice, and suffer for others. Pray that you can receive the Grace to let others serve, sacrifice, and suffer for you.

Keeping Our Sights Set on What is Truly Important

From the Fall of 1980 until December of 1983 my wife, Ellie, and I lived in Houston where I was in Optometry School at the University of Houston. We were 600 miles away from home and family for the first time in our married lives. In the Fall of 1982 I entered the third year of Optometry School. Third year was promoted as the most difficult of the four years of school. Fall of 1982 was also the time that Ellie and I decided to try to get pregnant for our first child. We both hoped for a son, and having read that the sperm carrying the Y Chromosome (the "male" chromosome) need a little more potassium to help them compete more effectively in the race to reach the egg first, and knowing that bananas are a good source of potassium I feverously ate bananas. A banana for breakfast, a banana for lunch, a banana for dinner, and maybe even a banana for a bed time snack. Ellie quickly became pregnant, and I just as quickly stopped eating so many bananas!

As the pregnancy progressed, I became more and more anxious for a son. We did not have any testing done that would tell us the sex of the child Ellie carried in her womb, so all I had was the hope of a male child. I had hopes and dreams of all the things my son would be and do, and of all the things I would do with him. At the top of my list were baseball and Boy Scouts. I had played baseball as a boy, and as was common for boys in the 1960's, I had dreamed of being a Major League Baseball player. I could hit for average, I had good running speed, I was a good fielder, but I lacked a strong throwing arm. Thus, my dream of playing Major League was just that: a dream, never to be reality. In my hopes and dreams for a son, however, he would have all of the attributes necessary for a good baseball player. I had also been in the Boy Scout program, beginning in Cub Scouts and advancing all the way to Eagle Scout. I had loved the monthly campouts, and the yearly summer long term camp, especially when my dad would come along. In my plans for a son, he would be in Boy Scouts also, and we would go camping together and I would teach him to tie all kinds of useful knots. I also was looking forward to watching Ellie be a mother, the job she had wanted to do as long as she could remember. As a child she played mother to her dolls, now both of us were looking forward to her chance to be a mother to a living child, a son if God so willed. Such were the hopes and dreams, the plans that I was formulating in my head if we should be so fortunate as to have a son.

One of our neighbors was a medical student preparing to become an Ob-Gyn doctor. He suggested a doctor for Ellie to see through her pregnancy and delivery. This doctor, however, generally only accepted high-risk pregnancies. But, as good fortune would have it, he accepted Ellie since she was referred by one of his students. Her pregnancy proceeded quite normally, and as pregnant women do, she got quite large. At the same time, she truly glowed with the happiness that only an expectant mother can. My third year of school went well and went quickly. Summer came and I was assigned to the clinic for the summer.

Ellie's due date came and went. She continued to grow larger, and less and less comfortable, and the summer Houston heat did not help. But the "pregnant glow of happiness" remained never the less. A week after her due date, we went to an afternoon movie, and then retired early to bed. About 11PM a soft sounding noise awakened me as if a cork had been popped from a wine bottle. Almost immediately I felt wetness in the bed. Ellie was awakened by the wetness, and we were both unsure at first what was going on. We both reacted with a "what the heck?" type of response. Then she said, "I think my water just broke!" Indeed it had. We frantically got out of bed, she showered, and I pulled the sheets off of the bed and threw them into the laundry. Together we gathered our "ready bag", called the doctor, and rushed to the hospital.

Her labor began quickly, and her pain increased quickly. I tried to help her stay as comfortable and relaxed as possible, trying to remember the different breathing patterns that we had learned together in Lamaze classes. I was not the best "coach". Should I be guiding her to use the "he-he-hoo" breathing pattern, or one of the other patters that I was struggling to recall? It did not seem to matter; no breathing pattern seemed to help ease her pain and discomfort. I watched the monitor for evidence of each coming contraction, and would prepare her, saying "here comes another one, get ready now, PUSH!" After several hours of this, Ellie had evidently had enough. When I said "PUSH", she responded "NO, I am not going to push any more!" I tried to be as positive as I could, saying, "OK, we missed that one, we'll get the next one". The nurse gave Ellie some medicine to relax her, and relax her it did; she looked at me with the first smile of the night, and said, "I see two of you." Meanwhile the doctor was becoming concerned because the baby had moved into the birth canal, and would move forward with each push, only to withdraw after the push. The baby just could not get out of the birth canal. He said the baby was too far down to do a C-Section now. He would have to do a Vaginal Section. He quickly gave Ellie local anesthetic, and began cutting. At 8:30AM, using forceps to grasp the baby's head, he pulled the baby out.

"You have a baby boy!" the doctor exclaimed. The nurse first gave the baby to Ellie so she could hold him. There is no more beautiful sight in the world than the look of complete love and devotion on the face of a mother holding her newborn child for the first time. The pain that Ellie had suffered, and the difficulties of labor and delivery vanished from her face as she held our first child, the son that we had been dreaming of. Then the nurse handed our baby son to me. His eyes were wide open and appeared to be looking all around, surveying the new world he had just discovered. Then I noticed the shape of his head. His skull was deformed, quite elongated and coming to a blunted point much like a cone with a rounded top. The shape reminded me of the "Saturday Night Live" characters, the Cone-Heads. Just as quickly, the nurse took our son away, and the doctor announced he was taking Ellie to surgery to repair the damage done by the difficult delivery and the Vaginal Section. I was ushered to the surgical waiting room.

Using the available phone, I called my parents and Ellie's parents to let them know of the birth of their newest grandson. Then I sat there, alone. I don't remember ever feeling as alone as I did at that time. My wife had been taken away, with very little explanation, to surgery. My newborn son had a deformed skull, and had also been taken away with little explanation. I sat there alone while family was 600 miles away, not knowing what was happening to my wife, or what it meant that my son had a deformed head. I thought of my mother, whose own mother had died from childbirth complications shortly after giving birth to her. I thought of my mother growing up never knowing her mother, and of mom's dad being suddenly forced to be a single parent. Sitting alone and feeling completely abandoned, with no one to comfort me, with my head in my hands, suddenly all of the hopes, dreams and plans that I had formulated for my son, and my wife and I, were not important. All I wanted now was much simpler. I only wanted the newborn son I had so anticipated to be OK. And I wanted Ellie, the love of my life, to be OK. That is all I wanted and prayed for at that moment: for them both to be OK. Just OK. Nothing fancy, just plain and simple OK. Such a simple wish compared to the grand plans that had been swirling in my head for the past 9 months.

It was almost noon when a nurse came to tell me that I could join Ellie in the surgery recovery room. She also informed me that they had given Ellie a spinal block during surgery, and that her legs were temporarily paralyzed and would require her to remain in recovery for several hours, at least until Ellie could walk again. By mid-afternoon she began to wiggle her toes, then her feet and eventually she could bend her knees. Later in the afternoon she was able to walk, although as she described, "it feels like I am walking on stubs." I began to have some good hopes for the future again; Ellie was going to be OK.

We did not get to see our newborn son again until later that evening. His head was already beginning to re-shape and loose the cone-head appearance (which, it turned out, was caused by the forceps used to grasp his head and drag him out of the birth canal). Now my son was going to be OK.

It did not take long for me to start dreaming of all the things that we would do as a family again; or all of the baseball my son, Charlie, and I would enjoy; or the Scouting adventures we would undertake together. The roller coaster ride of my dreams and hopes had transformed from grand to simple, and then back to grand again.

Three months later Ellie had to be hospitalized for complications related to the traumatic childbirth. I had started the final year of my training, and was expected to be at school, in class or in the clinic, from 8AM to 5PM Monday through Friday. There was no way that would be possible with Ellie in the hospital and a 3-month-old baby at home unless I had help. Family was still 600 miles away, but Ellie's mom came to Houston to help. She stayed in our small apartment with the baby while I went to school, and then in the evening we would all go to the hospital to visit Ellie. Her mom still had kids at home herself, so could not stay indefinitely. Once it became apparent that Ellie would need prolonged hospitalization, we realized that her mom would need to go home. So my sister, who had a one-year-old son at home herself, came to Houston to help. Still I hoped that Ellie would be released soon and we could go back to being a family again. Release from the hospital, however, was not to be soon. My sister needed to go back to her own family. Giving in to the hopeless uncertainty of the situation, I allowed my sister to take four month old Charlie back home with her to Wichita. There, he would be surrounded by family: my parents, Ellie's parents, and my sister. They would take turns keeping Charlie and caring for him until Ellie and I were able to do it again. Returning back to the apartment after taking my sister and Charlie to the airport for their flight to Wichita, I was once again alone. I felt lost, and any future I had planned in my dreams was now only an uncertainty. My family seemed to be falling apart. The quiet of the apartment without wife and son was overwhelming. My thoughts became dark. I had hit rock bottom. Would I be a single parent? Would Ellie recover? Once again, my grand plans, hopes and dreams seemed unimportant. Once again, all I wanted, all I prayed for was for Ellie to be OK. Shortly before Thanksgiving, after having spent more than 6 weeks in the hospital, Ellie was released. Unfortunately, she continued to need care and could not be left alone while I went to school each day. We immediately got a flight home to Wichita so Ellie could be reunited with our son, Charlie. She would have lots of help and attention from family to aid in her continued recovery. I returned to Houston, and in mid December packed our belongings with the help of two of Ellie's brothers. After a long all night drive, I was back in Wichita, hugging Ellie and holding Charlie once again.

Three years later Ellie became pregnant again, and my mind, once again, went completely wild with hopes and dreams of another child. Perhaps we would have another son, a brother for our first child. Twice the fun playing catch in the back yard, and twice the outdoor Scouting adventures! Twice the opportunity to watch my amazing wife be a truly magnificent mother! In February, Clint was born. This time the delivery went very smoothly, and both mother and baby were in good health right from the start. That evening I brought Charlie to the hospital to meet his new brother. I could hardly contain the excitement I held in my mind and heart for the future that our family had in front of us.

The next morning, Charlie woke and after getting out of bed he immediately fell to the floor. Trying to get up, he cried in pain "my knee hurts." He was able to get up, but walking was painful and he limped badly. I remembered that Ellie had told me that he had been limping some in the mornings recently. A trip to the doctor that morning for evaluation and x-rays resulted in Charlie being referred to a pediatric orthopedic specialist. Several weeks later, after having a bone scan, Charlie was diagnosed as having Perthes Disease. This is a rare childhood disease characterized by avascular necrosis of the bones in the hip socket. For some reason, the blood supply to one hip is decreased, causing the bones of the hip and femur to begin to soften. It can be temporary, but requires specialized leg braces to hold the legs outwards at 45-degree angles to prevent the hip socket from flattening out. This way, when the blood supply becomes re-established and the bones harden, the weight bearing parts of the hip socket will not have become deformed. Now seeing my 3-½ year old son wearing leg braces, my hopes and dreams for him were once again made unimportant. Again, my hopes and dreams were forced into re-evaluation. Once again, all I wanted for my son was that he be OK. All I wanted was for him to be able to walk without leg braces. A year later, a bone scan showed the bones to have good blood flow again, and the weight bearing parts of the hip to be shaped normally. The leg braces were removed, and Charlie could walk without the aid of leg braces. Predictably, it would seem, I soon began to entertain grand hopes and dreams for my family.

Each of our three sons would have physical problems that forced me to re-evaluate my grand plans for their lives. Charlie had fought and defeated Perthes Disease. Clint would have hearing problems that caused some of his coaches to complain that he did not listen to them. He simply could not hear them. In his teen-age years he developed severe acne. The medicine that he took did wonders for the acne, but it caused him to have severe joint pain that began to limit his athletic performance. Cliff developed a lazy eye, which required surgery and visual training. As a result, he did not have normal depth perception in his vision. Thus, sports such as baseball would be much more difficult, if not impossible, for him to excel in. Each of the boys did play some baseball, however only just enough to appease me. God did see fit to bless me with three sons who enjoyed Scouts, and a wife who supported each of them all the way to Eagle Scout.

There is an old saying: "If you want to make God laugh, tell him your plans!" I propose a slight modification to that saying, perhaps an addendum to it: "If you want to make God fall off of his chair laughing, tell him the plans you are making for other people!" That is exactly what I was doing with all of my grand plans, hopes and dreams that I was planning for my sons. Every time I began to take my plans too seriously, God threw up a roadblock to them, forcing me to re-evaluate those plans. I think he was trying to remind me that there are things much more important than the plans that I had formed in my mind. His roadblocks forced me to simplify my dreams so as to conform them to what is truly important. Simple things such as having a normal shaped head, or being able to walk without leg-braces, or hearing normally, or being able to run without joint pain, or having normal depth perception. God was reminding me that our health is more important than the dreams I had for my sons. He was also reminding me that I should love my sons and my wife as He had made them, not as I hoped them to be.

Ellie recovered from childbirth complications, although years later would undergo 2 surgical procedures to correct lingering problems that likely resulted from the trauma of the first delivery. Each of my sons excelled in sports, but none of the three enjoyed baseball. All three enjoyed soccer, so I learned to love soccer myself. I even helped as an assistant coach for their High School Soccer team. Charlie was a State Medalist in Wrestling. Clint was an All City Soccer player in High School, and was an All Conference Defender in College Soccer. Cliff was a 2 time State Medalist in High School Cross Country, and earned All Conference Honors in College Cross Country.

God's ways are not our ways. God's thoughts are not our thoughts. He was telling me in His own way that He had different plans for my family, and that I should stay focused on more important things than my family plans; things such as love and health. Instead of granting my wish for baseball loving sons, he gave me sons who enjoyed other sports. Instead of giving my sons and my wife perfect health, he gave each of them physical challenges that forced me to retreat from my grand family plans and move toward praying for a simpler, more important wish. We can and should have hopes and dreams, but at the same time we must remember to focus on things that are more important, things that truly matter: among them are good health and loving relationships.

Survivor's Guilt

Both my dad and his mother had colon cancer. That fact meant that I was at higher risk for colon cancer than the general population. Therefore, at age 41 I began having colon cancer screenings. That meant that I would go through a colonoscopy at the recommended frequency of every five years.

My first colonoscopy went well enough, no problems were found. The surgeon, however, said that I suffered "a particularly painful procedure". If you have ever had a colonoscopy you know that you have virtually no memory of the procedure. The anesthesiologist gives you the anesthesia, and the next thing you know is that you are waking up in recovery. I don't know what it meant that I had "a particularly painful procedure". Did I cry like a baby? Did I scream out in pain? I would just as soon not know the answer to those questions, so I did not ask the surgeon for details. I only hope that I maintained some degree of dignity.

The next two colonoscopies both revealed small polyps, which were removed during the procedure. Somehow, when it came time for my fourth colonoscopy, I missed the five-year mark, and it was not until six years that I had the procedure. It was the year 2010, and I was 57

years old when I had that fourth colonoscopy. When I awoke in the recovery room, the surgeon came in to inform me as to the results. He told me that there was a mass in my ascending colon, that at this time he did not know if it was cancerous or not. Either way, he said, I needed surgery to remove the ascending colon. Then he said,
"But first we have to figure out what is wrong with your heart."

While preparing me for anesthesia, the anesthesiologist had noticed that my EKG (heart rhythm) was abnormal. However, since I did not seem to be in any distress, he allowed the procedure to continue, monitoring the EKG closely for change. He advised the surgeon that before any further surgical procedure could be performed, a cardiologist would have to give approval.

I spent the next two months going through various heart tests. The cardiologist explained that he believed that I had an electrical problem that was causing the heart to beat abnormally. Since I was not having any symptoms, he approved the colon surgery provided that it must be performed at a major hospital with a cardiac care unit. Eventually, he said, I might require a pacemaker.

Soon after receiving approval from the cardiologist, I saw the colon surgeon and he explained the surgery that he would perform. He told me that if everything went well, I would not have to have a colostomy bag and would not have to have chemotherapy after surgery; although both were possibilities.

Three months after the colonoscopy, I finally had the surgery to remove my ascending colon. The surgery went well, and I did not need a colostomy bag. The final pathology report showed the mass to be pre-cancerous, having not penetrated beyond the colon wall and having not spread into any of the nearby lymph nodes. Recovery went well and after a few months, other than the scars, I could not tell that I had been through surgery.

During my recover, I learned that one of my acquaintances had undergone the same surgery 6 weeks after mine. About two years later another acquaintance went through the same surgery. Today, neither of them is with us anymore, having only survived a few years after their surgeries. Each of their masses was found too late. Both were found to have spread beyond the colon and into the lymph nodes.

Now I am left wondering why I was spared. Why was I fortunate enough to have my mass found while it was still pre-cancerous? What would have happened if I had not been a year late for my colonoscopy? Would there have been a mass one year earlier? If not, what would the outcome have been if the mass had not been found for another four years? Why are my friends gone, and I remain? Of course, these are questions that cannot be answered with certainty.

Yet, I ask them anyway. I began pondering the questions when the first friend passed. Then, when the second friend passed, the questions became more pressing. At times I feel a bit of guilt that I survived, and they did not. I know, it is not rational that I should feel guilt from this. I did nothing to contribute to the demise of my friends. I did nothing to give myself an advantage over them, creating an unfair playing ground. I did not cause their illness anymore than I caused my own. I did nothing to affect the outcome of their illness any more than I did my own. Each of us had a colonoscopy and was discovered to have a mass in our colon. Each of us had surgery to remove the mass and the involved section of colon. Yet our outcomes from that point were much different. I remain, and they do not. Because I am still here and they are not, I feel guilty. Even though there is no rationality to my feeling, I do feel guilty.

The guilt forces me to return to the question of why. Why do I survive and they do not? The only answers lie in faith. The answer cannot be found in a search for punishment and/or reward. My friends were not punished; nor is my survival a reward of any kind. Our creator created each of us in His image and likeness. We were given the gift of life and breath. In the same way, our creator decides when each of our lives is to end. It is His decision as to when our life on earth ends. Why He chose to end the lives of my friends while leaving me to survive is not for me to know. I must accept that He had His reasons, and that His ways are not my ways and His thoughts are not my thoughts. My faith leads me to believe that when it is my turn to leave this life I will enter into the presence of God, my creator. When that day comes, I will see clearly. I will know the answers to the questions that vex me today. Until that day, I must hold onto that faith and hope that one day my questions will be answered. Meanwhile, the questions remain, and the irrational feelings of guilt continue. I must do my best every day to live as He wants me to live; striving to do His will every day; hoping with faith that one day I will hear the words "Well done my good and faithful servant", and my questions will be answered, bringing an end to the feelings of guilt.

Be a Duck

In writing this chapter, I am going to deviate from the original plan of the book. I am not going to relate any stories from my life that led to my learning this particular lesson. Rather, I am simply going to explain the lesson.

Throughout my life I have encountered people who did not like me. In this regard, I am not unique. We all are faced with the fact that there are persons who do not like us. The realization that a particular person does not like us can be quite discomforting because we all want to be liked. We all want everyone to like us. The truth is that everyone does not like me. I suspect that there has never been, and never will be, a person who is universally liked. Such is the nature of humanity.

So, the question is what to do about this fact. Sometimes it is easy for me to reconcile another's dislike, simply because I do not like that person either. It is much more difficult to accept dislike when it comes from a person who I really want to like me. How can I make that person like me? What can I do so that he or she will like me?

I have learned that I cannot make another person like me. How did I learn that? By observing that another person cannot make me like them. I cannot say to another person, "You have to like me!" or "You have to stop insulting me" and make them suddenly like me or stop the insults. I cannot change a single thing about another person. I can only change myself. I can try to understand what it is about me that another person does not like, and then I can try to change that in me. Thus, by making change in myself, I can indirectly affect change in another.

Sometimes, however, despite my own efforts to affect change, I fail. The person that I really want to like me continues to dislike me for his or her own reasons. That is life. The question remains, what to do in the face of this dislike, how to respond to dislike or insult.

The answer is found indirectly in something that Eleanor Roosevelt said. "No one can make you feel inferior without your consent." One of the reasons that it bothers me when another person does not like me is that it makes me feel inferior. It makes me feel that I am not good enough somehow. I have realized that, just as Eleanor Roosevelt said, when I let another person's dislike for me to make me feel inferior, it is only because I have allowed it. I have given my consent. So what do I do? I become a duck. I let it all roll off my back like water off a duck's back.

You may hear others talk about being "thick skinned" or "thin skinned". A person who is "thin skinned" is easily bothered by insult or dislike. A person who is "thick skinned" is not so easily bothered, because the "thick skin" is hard to penetrate. This implies, to some extent, that a person is either "thick skinned" or is "thin skinned" and does not have a choice in the matter. I prefer to think in terms of becoming a duck. I can choose to be like a duck, and to let insult and dislike roll off my back like water off a duck's back. I have complete control over my response to dislike or insult. I cannot change the other person. I can only change myself. It is a matter of choice, I can give my consent or not. I can choose to be a duck or not to be a duck. When I become like a duck, I remove my consent. How I respond is up to me. It is a choice I make. I choose to respond by becoming like a duck.

Who Am I?

After 34 years of working as an optometrist, I retired. As the retirement date grew closer and closer, I began to ask myself the question: When I no longer do what I do, who will I be? Put another way, when I stop being an eye doctor, who will I be? As I got closer and closer to retirement, I could sense that question haunting me more and more. I could sense a darkness looming ahead if I did not come to a reasonable answer to that question. You see, I had been seeing my identity in terms of what I do; not in terms of who I am. Too often in society, our identities are determined by what we do, rather than by whom we are. When that happens, we can lose sight of who we are, just as I had done. Fortunately, I came to an answer to the question I pondered, without falling into the abyss of darkness and despair that is so easy to fall into, yet so hard to climb out of.

In Genesis 1:1, the Bible says "In the beginning God created the heavens and the earth." Then, on the sixth day he said "Let us make man in our image" (Genesis 1:26). Notice that he did not say, "Let me make man in my image." Why not? The answer lies in who God is: God the Father, God the Son, and God the Holy Spirit. We believe that God is a triune God: three persons in one God. God's identity is determined by relationship, the relationship of the Father to the Son, the Son to the Father, and the Spirit to each. That is who God is. It is not what God is, or what God does. What God is can be found in what God did. He created the heavens and the earth. That makes him the creator. But notice that after six days of creating, God rested. I interpret that to mean that after six days of creating he retired. That is not to say that he stopped doing, he just retired from creating the heavens and the earth. He was still and will always be, the Father-Son-Holy Spirit. He simply no longer did what he had done, creating the heavens and the earth. He continued to serve each of us by guiding our lives, unseen. Nudging us in a new direction when we stray. Now and then allowing us to see ourselves through His eyes. Teaching us how we should live our lives. He authored a book, the Bible, which has many stories providing us with examples of other people's lives, and the manner in which they lived and the lessons they learned along the way. God intended that we should learn from those life stories and examples so as to better live our own lives.

Since we were created in the image of God, we were created for relationship, just as He is relationship. We are children of God. He created us to know, love, and serve Him. In doing so we know, love, and serve each other. That is what we do, it is not who we are. What we do is merely a reflection of who we are. We should not make the mistake of allowing what we do to be the determinate of who we are. Remember, we are first and foremost His children. As an eye doctor, I served others by providing eye care, helping people see better, diagnosing and treating eye disease. That is only what I did. That is not who I was, or who I am. Just as God retired from creating the heavens and the earth, I retired from being an eye doctor. And just as God continued being who he was, so too will I continue being who I was. I continue to serve others, but in different ways.

Now we go back to the question I posed earlier: "When I stop being an eye doctor, who will I be?" The answer lies in the fact that we were created in the image of God, we were created for relationship. Having come to an answer, I am now at peace.

I am Chuck Kissling, a child of God, a son, a brother, a husband, a father, a father in law, a grandfather, and a friend.

Afterword

We all hope that somehow our lives make a difference in the world. I am no different. I hope that my life has made a difference in the lives of others, at least in the life of one other person. Perhaps, even, that the lessons I have described in my stories might make a difference or be helpful in the life of you the reader. If, and I stress if, I have made any difference in our world, it is because of the Grace of God, and the people who have been present in my life and who have helped to shape and form me into the person I am. I am referring to people such as those in my stories: my grandparents, my parents, my siblings, my spouse, my children, and my friends. Any difference I may have made in this world is only because of the involvement of others in my life; and because of the difference that they made in my life. For all of these people, and the impact that they have had on my life, I am eternally grateful.

About the Author

Charles W. Kissling (Chuck) was born in 1953 in Bartlesville, Oklahoma, the son of Ira and Mary Kissling, and the oldest of three children. He began school in Bartlesville, then the family moved to Winfield, Kansas. One year later they moved to Wichita, Kansas, where they lived until 1969 before moving to White Bear Lake, Minnesota.

Charles graduated from White Bear High School, and then attended the University of Minnesota, graduating in 1976 with a Bachelor of Elected Studies with the emphasis in Genetics and Cell Biology. He moved back to Wichita, where he attended Medical Technology School at St. Francis Hospital. After becoming a Registered Medical Technologist he worked in the Blood Bank doing research. He was the co-author of research articles that were published in two different international medical journals. In 1980 he entered Optometry School at the University of Houston, graduating in 1984 with the degree Doctor of Optometry.

Chuck and his wife, Ellie, raised 3 sons and were active in their church, school, Cub Scouts and Boy Scouts, soccer, wrestling, cross country and baseball. The oldest son (Charlie) played one year of college Soccer, then joined the Marine Corps and saw combat in Iraq. He graduated from college, and works as Environmental Health and Safety Administrator; he is married and has 9 children. The middle son (Clint) played 4 years of college Soccer, graduated from college and works in IT for a major hospital company; he is married and has one child. The youngest son (Cliff) ran college Cross Country four years, attended Medical School and is a physician; he is married and has 2 children.

After practicing Optometry in Wichita for 34 years, Chuck retired. He now stays busy with church activities, travel, home projects, and enjoying having time to spend with his wife, his sons and their wives, and with the grandchildren.